THE ALTAR BREAKER

Unlocking the Secrets to Deliverance and Spiritual Freedom

MONICA DAVIS

Copyright © 2025 Monica Davis. All rights reserved.

Published and designed by Ministry Event Marketing.

Printed in the United States of America

ISBN: 979-8-9986757-0-6 Paperback

ISBN: 979-8-9986757-1-3 Hardback

Disclaimer This publication is designed to provide accurate and authoritative information regarding the subject matter covered. All materials are the intellectual property of the Monica Davis Living Trust.

No part of this book may be reproduced, stored in a retrieval system, or transmitted in any form or by any means, electronic, mechanical, photocopying, recording, or otherwise, without express written permission of the author or publisher except by a reviewer who may quote brief passages in a review.

Unauthorized distribution, sale, or resale of any such property will result in legal action to compensate the trust for the unauthorized use of its private property.

Scriptures marked NIV are taken from the NEW INTERNATIONAL VERSION (NIV): Scripture taken from THE HOLY BIBLE, NEW INTERNATIONAL VERSION ®. Copyright© 1973, 1978, 1984, 2011 by Biblica, Inc.™. Used by permission of Zondervan.

Scripture taken from the New King James Version®. Copyright © 1982 by Thomas Nelson. Used by permission. All rights reserved.

Scriptures marked KJV are taken from the KING JAMES VERSION (KJV): KING JAMES VERSION, public domain.

CONTENTS

Dedication 7

Acknowledgments 9

Preface 11

Introduction 17

Part 1: The Foundation of Bondage

- Chapter 1: Unlocking the Secrets of Demonic Altars 3
- Chapter 2: Spiritual Legalities: Understanding the Laws of Altars ... 19
- Chapter 3: How Demonic Altars Are Built to Bind You 33

Part 2: Breaking the Chains of Darkness

- Chapter 4: Breaking Free: Identifying Demonic Altars in Your Life and Bloodline. 45
- Chapter 5: The Battle Plan: Spiritual Warfare and the Power of Prayer . .. .57
- Chapter 6: Destroying Demonic Altars: Step-by-Step Spiritual Victory. 71
- Chapter 7: Ancestral and Territorial Altars: Breaking Generational Strongholds 83

Part 3: Rising in Power and Dominion

- Chapter 8: Total Freedom: Deliverance and Maintaining Your Spiritual Victory.................................95
- Chapter 9: Rebuilding Godly Altars: Establishing Divine Foundations 107
- Chapter 10: Living in Unshakable Spiritual Victory 117
- Definitions 129
- Appendix A: Quick Reference Guide to Prayers for Deliverance...133
- Appendix B: Quick Reference Prophetic Declarations & Activation Prayers...153

DEDICATION

To my beloved daughters,
Jahraeona & Rayvin,

This book is not just a collection of words; it is a birth, a travail, and a manifestation of pain turned into purpose. Just as a mother endures labor to bring forth life, I endured spiritual labor pains to bring forth the revelations within these pages. There were moments I had to push when I had no strength left, moments where the weight of the battle seemed unbearable. And yet, even without fully understanding, you both were there—laboring with me in your way, standing in the fire with me as I fought to break the chains that sought to bind our family.

This journey was not just my sacrifice; it was yours, too. You endured seasons of uncertainty, seasons of lack, and seasons of breaking while watching me press through trials that neither of us could always comprehend. But know that every tear, every trial, every battle was not in vain. This book is a testimony that deliverance is authentic, that generational curses can be broken, and that freedom belongs to us.

I am forever grateful for your love, resilience, and silent strength. I pray these words become a guiding light for you, equipping you with the wisdom and power to walk in deliverance and establish a new legacy with freedom, healing, and divine purpose.

With all my love,
Mommy

ACKNOWLEDGEMENTS

First and foremost, I give all honor, glory, and praise to God, my Deliverer, my Strength, and my Teacher. It is by His wisdom, grace, and power that this book was birthed. Every revelation, every lesson, every victory came through You. Without your divine guidance, I would not have had the strength to endure the process that led to these pages.

To my daughters, Jahraeona & Rayvin, your love, patience, and sacrifice have not gone unnoticed. This journey was not mine alone; you endured with me. Even in moments when you did not understand, you stood by me. You are my greatest blessings, and I dedicate this work to you so that you may walk in the freedom I fought to obtain.

To my family and close friends who covered me in prayer, encouraged me when I wanted to give up, and reminded me of my assignment, thank you. Your unwavering support, whether in words, prayers, or simple acts of love, meant more than you will ever know.

To my Apostolic Covering, spiritual mother and father, spiritual midwives, spiritual mentors, and leaders who poured into me, challenged me, and helped shape me into the warrior I am today, I honor you. Your teachings and impartation gave me the strength and wisdom to press forward and fulfill my calling.

To every person who has ever sown into my life, whether through a word of encouragement, prayer, or simply believing in me, I see and appreciate you. Your support has helped push this book into existence.

To those who have battled in silence, who have struggled under the weight of generational curses, spiritual warfare, and hidden strongholds, this book was written for you. May these words be a weapon in your hands, equipping you to break free and walk in the sustained deliverance God has ordained for you.

Finally, to my future readers, thank you for allowing me to be part of your journey. This book will transform your life, deepen your faith, and lead you to victory.

With love and gratitude,
Monica Davis

PREFACE

In a world where spiritual forces constantly battle for dominion over lives, families, and territories, many unknowingly find themselves in deep spiritual bondage. Their struggles may manifest in relationships, finances, health, or mental and emotional well-being, yet the root cause of their suffering often remains hidden in the unseen realm. At the core of this spiritual entanglement are demonic altars—dark spiritual forces that gain legal ground to operate, disrupt, and destroy.

I am writing this book to expose and confront the demonic altars that operate in the shadows, influencing lives in ways that often go unnoticed. For too long, believers have fought the symptoms, unaware of the source of their spiritual oppression. My goal is to help you understand the spiritual realities of demonic altars and empower you to rise in your God-given authority to destroy them.

Throughout this book, we will delve deeply into topics such as how demonic altars are erected, the role they play in spiritual bondage, and how they influence generational curses, territorial strongholds, and personal struggles. I will guide you step-by-step in identifying demonic altars in your life—whether they stem from personal sin, ancestral ties, or cultural practices. We will also explore the vital importance of spiritual warfare, strategic prayer, and fasting as the weapons to break these altars and reclaim the freedom Jesus Christ has already won for you.

By reading this book, you will receive more than just knowledge; you will be equipped with practical spiritual tools to dismantle every demonic altar. You will learn how to break covenants, cancel demonic decrees, and call down the fire of God to destroy every stronghold. Most importantly, you will understand how to rebuild and maintain Godly altars that invite His presence, power, and protection into every area of your life.

As you engage with the truths in this book, I pray that you will walk in spiritual victory, free from the chains of demonic altars, and empowered to help others find their freedom. Together, we will declare war on the forces of darkness and destroy every demonic altar that has been erected against God's purpose for your life! It is time to break free and live in the abundant life Christ has promised.

Mount Zion is where deliverance is established, chains are broken, and the presence of the Lord reigns supreme. So,

Father, I ask You to let this book be a divine encounter with You—the One who transforms, enlightens, and sets us free! Father, speak through Your Word, and cause our eyes to be opened. Let every veil be lifted, every mystery unveiled, and every hidden truth be revealed. In Jesus' Mighty Name, and by the power of Your Word, grant me total liberty to deliver these truths, for it is written that:

***"You shall know the truth, and the truth shall make you free." –* John 8:31-32**

Deliverance Is the Children's Bread: A Believer's Inheritance

Deliverance is not a distant hope for the believer—it is your inheritance. It's not something you have to earn or beg for; it is a gift that belongs to you under your identity in Christ. Through His death and resurrection, Jesus made a way for you to walk in freedom, which is yours to claim as a child of God.

In **Matthew 15:26**, Jesus said, *"It is not good to take the children's bread and throw it to the dogs."*

He spoke to a Gentile woman who sought healing for her daughter, and He made it clear that deliverance, the "children's bread," belongs to the children of God. As a believer, this freedom, this deliverance, is your right. It's part of your inheritance.

You don't have to fight for deliverance like a distant promise; it's yours. Jesus paid for it. His victory over the enemy is your victory. In **1 John 3:8,** the Word says,

"For this purpose the Son of God was manifested, that He might destroy the works of the devil."

That includes every form of oppression, fear, sickness, and bondage. Everything that tries to hold you captive has already been defeated.

Jesus came to set you free. Deliverance is a part of the abundant life He promised. It's not just about physical healing or breaking chains in a moment—it's about walking in complete freedom, mind, body, and spirit.

When Jesus stood up and declared in **Luke 4:18,**

"The Spirit of the Lord is upon Me, because He has anointed Me to preach the gospel to the poor; He has sent Me to heal the brokenhearted, to proclaim liberty to the captives, and recovery of sight to the blind, to set at liberty those who are oppressed,"

He wasn't just talking about the oppressed in His time, He was talking about you. His mission is your mission. Deliverance is your inheritance in Christ and is available to you right now!

As you apply the spiritual principles in this book, these secrets of deliverance will lead you to sustainable, lasting freedom. This is not a temporary fix; it's a complete transformation. Through understanding and applying these biblical truths, you will walk in total freedom that lasts. It's not just about breaking free in the moment; it's about walking in victory every day, remaining free from the enemy's influence and strongholds. This kind of freedom is not just a one-time event but a lifelong journey.

So as you read this book, remember: deliverance is your inheritance as a believer. It's the children's bread. Through Jesus, you have the authority and the power to claim it. These spiritual truths will lead you into lasting, sustainable deliverance, empowering you to live fully in the freedom Christ has already secured.

INTRODUCTION

Have **you ever fasted**, prayed fervently, and declared the Word of God with unwavering faith, only to feel like you're still trapped in an endless cycle, waiting for a breakthrough that never comes? Despite your dedication and steadfast faith, do invisible barriers block your progress? No matter how hard you try, do specific negative patterns persist, leaving you frustrated and doubtful? Sometimes, it may even seem as if your faith and prayers are ineffective, making you question the very power of the Word or God.

Yet, the Bible teaches,

> ***"Through knowledge, the just will be delivered"***
> Proverbs 11:9

It is not enough to have good intentions or a sincere heart; understanding is essential. In my study on altars, I was amazed by how much I didn't know and how incomplete my understanding had been. I fought countless unseen battles for decades, yet never truly walked in complete victory. Yes, we boldly declare we have the victory, but many of us are still secretly waging unseen wars and living defeated lives behind closed doors.

"If you've been facing these persistent struggles, there may be a more profound, unseen force at work. One spiritual mystery has shaped destinies and determined outcomes throughout history: altars. Whether Godly or demonic, these spiritual structures can influence lives; unless confronted, they can keep you and your bloodline bound for generations.

The mystery of altars holds the secrets to breakthroughs, bondages, and spiritual dominion. To walk in victory, you must understand the systems governing divine and demonic altars. Lord, reveal the hidden wisdom of altars so that we may dismantle every structure that has hindered our progress and establish Godly altars that align with Your will for our lives!

In this kingdom, we do not rise by our efforts alone or human wisdom; we rise and reign through light. Light represents revelation, understanding, and divine insight. When God desires to elevate a man, He does not simply change his circumstances; He shortens the distance between him and the light required for his ascension. The mercy of God is often demonstrated by granting accelerated access to the revelation that shifts a man from bondage to dominion.

For it is written,

"The people that sat in darkness have seen a great light"

—**Matthew 4:16**

This light is not just information; it is the power that lifts, transforms destinies, and enforces kingdom rulership. The absence of light keeps men in captivity and bondage, but the presence of divine revelation causes kings to rise.

Lord, let Your light shine upon us today. Illuminate the path before us, expose every hidden snare and agenda from the enemy, and lead us into unshakable victory. Let the mysteries of Your kingdom be unlocked now, and may we walk in the fullness of our God-ordained authority. In Jesus' name, Amen!

What Is an Altar?

The Hebrew word for altar, *mizbeah* (מִזְבֵּחַ), which comes from the root word meaning "to slaughter," underscores the altar's role as a place of sacrifice. In the New Testament, the Greek term *thusiasterion* (θυσιαστήριον) is used, which refers to a place of sacrifice or offering. The altar represents a sacred space where offerings and spiritual transactions occur.

An altar is more than just a physical structure; it is a profound spiritual platform, a legal gateway through which the spirit realm connects with the physical world. Altars serve as places where both divine and demonic forces can interact with humanity, operating under specific legal grounds or permissions.

In **Luke 1:10-11**, we see a powerful example of this intersection: the altar becomes where heaven and earth align, allowing for divine intervention and communication.

> **10** *And the whole multitude of the people were praying outside at the hour of incense. 11 And there appeared to him an angel of the Lord standing on the right side of the altar of incense.*
>
> **— Luke 1:10-11**

At its core, an altar permits spiritual laws to operate on the earth. It is the legal gateway for spirits—whether good or evil—to function in the physical realm. God created the world as the domain for mankind, and according to the spiritual law of territory, no entity has the right to operate here without a physical body. Even God Himself abides by this law, as dominion was granted to spirits housed in human vessels. While spirits can inhabit and influence animals, they do not have dominion over the earth. That authority is reserved for those in human bodies who serve as vessels for manifesting spiritual power.

Altars are not just historical relics of ancient worship; they are a recurring and foundational theme in the Bible, appearing **378 times** throughout Scripture. This frequency underscores their spiritual significance, from the Old Testament patriarchs building altars to establish covenants with God to the New Testament's revelation of Christ as the ultimate sacrifice upon the altar of redemption.

Every altar carries a voice, a testimony in the spirit realm that calls for a response. Whether an altar is built by divine instruction or demonic influence, it is a spiritual anchor that enforces covenants, dictates patterns, and influences destinies. Understanding the function of altars is essential for anyone seeking true spiritual freedom, as these structures hold the legal grounds through which blessings or bondage flow into one's life.

The patriarchs of old understood these profound mysteries, so they operated in such superior levels of dominion on the earth. They recognized that altars are the key to unlocking spiritual authority and establishing lasting influence. Altars serve as legal access points for spiritual forces, both divine and demonic, to manifest and operate in the physical realm. Whether we realize it or not, altars influence many patterns, struggles, and breakthroughs we experience. They act as ongoing spiritual markers, allowing the power of the covenant they represent to persist even after those who built them are no longer physically present.

Yet, many of us remain unaware of how deeply altars shape our lives. These unseen structures impact everything—from personal behaviors to generational patterns, family struggles, and the rise and fall of entire nations. This book seeks to illuminate the hidden power of altars and reveal how they have influenced our lives for good and evil.

Restoring the True Biblical Understanding of Altars

Many believers struggle to fully grasp the concept of altars because, in today's time, the teaching of altars has often been shaped by prophetic and apostolic circles, sometimes in ways that lack a solid biblical foundation. While the reality of altars is deeply spiritual, how it has been communicated has sometimes caused friction, confusion, distortion, or even manipulation within the body of Christ.

Some have reduced altars to rituals, using them as tools for personal gain rather than teaching believers their true spiritual significance and biblical foundation. Unfortunately, this has led many to misunderstand or reject the concept altogether. However, just because a spiritual truth has been misrepresented does not mean it is unscriptural. Instead, it calls for us to return to the Word of God to properly understand what altars are, their purpose, and how they function in a believer's life.

As we examine the first mentions of the word *"altar"* in Genesis, we observe a clear and profound pattern that sets the foundation for how altars are understood in biblical terms. What stands out is that none of these early references to altars are connected to anything demonic or negative. Instead, the altars were built by godly men who deeply revered God and desired to honor Him. These altars were dedicated to God as sacred places for worship, covenant, and encounters with God.

Every time an altar was erected, it served a significant purpose:

- The altar became a sacred place where the worshiper **called upon the name of the Lord** in prayer and communion with Him.

- Altars were built to **honor significant acts** of God's intervention, whether it was a divine covenant, a blessing, or a moment of victory.

- Altars were also raised after **great hardships or disasters**, as a reminder of God's faithfulness and a mark of His deliverance from difficult circumstances.

Altars in the Book of Genesis: A Biblical Pattern

From the beginning of Scripture, altars emerge as a recurring theme among those who feared and served the true God. Every mention of an altar in Genesis is built by men of faith, signifying devotion, obedience, and a deep desire to encounter God.

- **Noah's Altar (Genesis 8:20-21)** – After the flood, Noah built an altar and offered a **sacrifice to God**, prompting God to establish a new covenant with humanity.

    20 Then Noah built an altar to the LORD and, taking some of all the clean animals and clean birds, he sacrificed burnt offerings on it. 21 The LORD smelled the pleasing aroma and said in his heart: "Never again will I curse the ground because of humans, even though[a] every inclination of the human heart is evil from childhood. And never again will I destroy all living creatures, as I have done.

    —Genesis 8:20-21

- **Abraham's Altars (Genesis 12:7-8, 13:4, 22:9-14)** Abraham built altars in various locations, signifying **worship, divine encounters, and covenant relationships** with God.

7 The Lord *appeared to Abram and said, "To your offspring[a] I will give this land." So he built an altar there to the* Lord, *who had appeared to him. 8 From there he went on toward the hills east of Bethel and pitched his tent, with Bethel on the west and Ai on the east. There he built an altar to the* Lord *and called on the name of the* Lord.

—Genesis 12:7-8

4 and where he had first built an altar. There Abram called on the name of the Lord.

—Genesis 13:4

9 When they reached the place God had told him about, Abraham built an altar there and arranged the wood on it. He bound his son Isaac and laid him on the altar, on top of the wood. 10 Then he reached out his hand and took the knife to slay his son. 11 But the angel of the Lord *called out to him from heaven, "Abraham! Abraham!"*

"Here I am," he replied.

12 "Do not lay a hand on the boy," he said. "Do not do anything to him. Now I know that you fear God, because you have not withheld from me your son, your only son."

13 Abraham looked up and there in a thicket he saw a ram[a] caught by its horns. He went over and took the ram and sacrificed it as a burnt offering instead of his son. 14 So Abraham called that place The L<small>ORD</small> Will Provide. And to this day it is said, "On the mountain of the L<small>ORD</small> it will be provided."

—-Genesis 22:9-14

- **Isaac's Altar (Genesis 26:25)** – Isaac built an altar as a place of **worship and surrender** to God.

25 Isaac built an altar there and called on the name of the L<small>ORD</small>. There he pitched his tent, and there his servants dug a well.

—Genesis 26:25

- **Jacob's Altar (Genesis 35:7)** – Jacob built an altar at Bethel, marking where he encountered God and reaffirming his commitment to Him.

> **7 There he built an altar, and he called the place El Bethel,[a] because it was there that God revealed himself to him when he was fleeing from his brother—Genesis 35:7**

In each of these instances, the altar was dedicated to the one true God, demonstrating faith, obedience, and covenant relationship. This pattern in Genesis sets a precedent that altars were never random or superstitious rituals. They were established by men who honored God.

Correcting The Misuse: The Danger of Ritualistic or Manipulative Teachings on Altars

While altars are biblical, there has been a misuse of the teaching on altars in some modern ministries. Some leaders have turned the concept into:

- A ritual rather than a revelation – Treating altars as ceremonial practices instead of spiritual realities.

- A tool for manipulation – Using fear-based teachings on altars to extract financial sacrifices from people.

- A mystical concept – Promoting unbiblical practices with no basis in Scripture, such as teaching that one must build physical altars to receive breakthroughs.

Actual biblical teaching on altars does not promote manipulation, superstition, or ritualistic sacrifices. Instead, it reveals how believers can:

✔ Understand **spiritual authority** through Christ's ultimate sacrifice.
✔ Break **demonic altars** and ungodly agreements.
✔ Establish a **strong foundation** of worship, prayer, and covenant with God.

The Call to Restore Sound Biblical Teaching on Altars

Because altars play a foundational role in spiritual life and warfare, they must be taught correctly. The enemy benefits when believers are ignorant or misinformed about altars because he understands their power and legality in the spiritual realm.

Just as in the days of Genesis, altars today must be understood as:

- A place of **worship and surrender** to the true God.
- A point of **covenant and divine encounter** with the Lord.
- A means of **establishing spiritual authority** in a believer's life.

- A battlefield where **spiritual victories are won**.

The goal is not to abandon the teaching of altars but to restore it to its biblical foundation, ensuring that believers can walk in **truth, deliverance, and spiritual authority** without falling into manipulation or false teachings.

Conclusion

Altars play a pivotal role in both the spiritual and physical realms. They are platforms where covenants are activated, patterns are established, and spiritual laws are enforced. Understanding the power and function of altars is crucial for breaking free from negative patterns and stepping into the fullness of God's promises.

If you've ever found yourself battling the same cycles, struggling with unseen resistance, or feeling like something invisible is working against your progress, the answer may lie in an ancient biblical mystery overlooked by many: the power of spiritual altars.

Nothing in the spiritual realm happens without a legal right, and altars serve as the courtrooms where verdicts are rendered, destinies are determined, and spiritual agreements are either reinforced or broken. Whether established knowingly or unknowingly, altars dictate the flow of blessings or curses in our lives. This is why breakthroughs often seem delayed or denied—an existing altar speaks against what God has declared over you.

But here's the good news: **no demonic altar is greater than the power of the Cross.** Just as altars can bind, they can also be broken. Just as they enforce curses, they can be dismantled to establish blessings. In the chapters ahead, we will uncover the hidden influence of altars in our lives, expose the enemy's tactics, and walk through the divine strategy for dismantling every ungodly altar working against you.

It's time to take back your spiritual authority. It's time to silence the altars speaking against your destiny.

Let's begin…

Closing Prayer: Breaking the Power of Unseen Altars

Heavenly Father,

I come before You in the name of Jesus Christ, acknowledging that You alone are the true and living God. You are the Alpha and the Omega, the God of covenant, and the Ruler of heaven and earth. Lord, I thank You for revealing spiritual altars and their influence on my life. I ask that you open my eyes to discern the unseen structures that have shaped my patterns, decisions, and destiny.

Father, if there are any ungodly altars in my life—altars erected through my lineage, my actions, or by the enemy—I renounce them now in Jesus' name. I break every legal right they hold over me, my family, and my bloodline. By the power of the blood of Jesus, I sever every demonic covenant, decree, and agreement that has been established against my destiny. Let every altar speaking against my purpose be silenced now!

Lord, I ask You to establish Your divine altar in my life. Let my body, home, and heart become a holy dwelling for Your presence. I surrender every area of my life to You and declare that Jesus Christ is the ultimate sacrifice—His blood has redeemed me from every curse, and I now walk in the freedom and authority of Your kingdom.

Holy Spirit, teach me how to build a life that glorifies You. Let my worship, prayers, and obedience become an altar of righteousness before You. May my life be a testimony of Your power, favor, and deliverance.

I declare that from this day forward, I am free. The chains of the past are broken, and I step into the fullness of my God-ordained destiny. In Jesus' mighty name, **Amen.**

Part 1
The Foundation of Bondage

CHAPTER 1:
Unlocking The Secrets Of Demonic Altars

Altars are spiritual gateways, portals that connect the natural and spiritual realms. Throughout Scripture, altars are mentioned as places of worship, sacrifice, and covenant. While Godly altars invite God's presence and power, demonic altars serve as access points for darkness, bondage, and destruction. The enemy erected these altars to establish strongholds in the lives of individuals, families, regions, and even entire nations.

Understanding demonic altars is essential for believers who desire spiritual freedom and victory. These altars are often at the root of persistent struggles—generational curses, unexplainable cycles of failure, sickness, and oppression. Many people battle unseen forces without realizing that a spiritual contract was established against them through these altars. In this chapter, we will uncover the mysteries of demonic altars, their purpose, how they operate in the unseen realm, and how they infiltrate lives undetected realm, and how they can infiltrate a person's life undetected.

Demonic Altars: The Kingdom of Darkness' Strongholds

The kingdom of darkness establishes demonic altars to advance Satan's agenda on the earth. These altars are erected through sin, idolatry, witchcraft, and other ungodly practices, giving demonic forces legal access to bring destruction, bondage, and curses into people's lives.

Biblical Examples of Demonic Altars

- **Altars of Baal Worship**

    In the Old Testament, Baal worship was a significant idolatry that invited demonic influence over individuals and territories. When God called Gideon, one of his first assignments was to destroy his father's altar to Baal:

25 That same night, the LORD said to him, "Take the second bull from your father's herd, the one seven years old. Tear down your father's altar to Baal and cut down the Asherah pole beside it. 26 Then build a proper kind of altar to the LORD your God on the top of this height. Using the wood of the Asherah pole that you cut down, offer the second bull as a burnt offering."

27 So Gideon took ten of his servants and did as the LORD told him. But because he was afraid of his family and the townspeople, he did it at night rather than in the daytime.

28 In the morning, when the people of the town got up, there was Baal's altar, demolished, with the Asherah pole beside it cut down and the second bull sacrificed on the newly built altar!

—**Judges 6:25-28**

This passage illustrates that the demonic altar had to be torn down before Gideon could lead Israel to victory.

- **Altars of Ancestral Rituals and Blood Sacrifice**

Demonic altars can also be established through ancestral rituals, bloodshed, and occult practices. God warned His people against engaging in such sacrifices:

7 They must no longer offer any of their sacrifices to the goat idols to whom they prostitute themselves. This is to be a lasting ordinance for them and for the generations to come.'

—**Leviticus 17:7**

The Power and Influence of Demonic Altars

Demonic altars thrive on sin and disobedience, creating spiritual strongholds that bind and oppress. Sin fuels these altars, allowing them to strengthen and exert greater control over individuals, families, and entire regions. The more sin and rebellion persist, the more these altars gain power, feeding on the negative energy generated by disobedience to divine laws. In the spiritual realm, they serve as chains of bondage, trapping souls in cycles of destruction, despair, and stagnation.

The Nature of Demonic Altars

Demonic altars are spiritual platforms established by the kingdom of darkness, where sacrifices and covenants are made to empower demonic forces. These altars provide the enemy with **legal grounds** to operate in the lives of individuals, families, and territories. Unlike physical altars that can be seen and touched, demonic altars are often unseen but no less real. They serve as meeting points where demonic spirits engage with humans through rituals, sacrifices, and spiritual agreements.

Scripture Reference:
"But I say that the things which the Gentiles sacrifice, they sacrifice to devils, and not to God."
—1 Corinthians 10:20

The Bible provides clear examples of altars being used to establish both divine and demonic covenants. In *1 Kings 18,* Elijah confronted the prophets of Baal on Mount Carmel, where they had erected an altar to their false god. This altar became a gateway for demonic power to influence the people, drawing strength from the realm of darkness.

The Spiritual Mechanics of Altars

1. Sacrifices Empower Altars

Every altar requires a sacrifice to remain active. On Godly altars, these sacrifices include prayer, worship, and obedience to God. Conversely, demonic altars are fueled by sin, bloodshed, and ungodly rituals, which empower the forces of darkness.

2. Covenants Are Established at Altars

Altars serve as places of spiritual agreements. Covenants at altars can knowingly or unknowingly affect individuals, families, and entire generations.

3. Altars Shape Natural Outcomes

What happens at an altar determines spiritual atmospheres, which, in turn, influence events in the physical world. Godly altars release blessings, breakthroughs, and divine protection, while demonic altars enforce oppression, stagnation, and setbacks.

4. Altars Require Ongoing Maintenance

Both Godly and demonic altars must be maintained. Godly altars thrive through prayer, worship, and righteous living, while demonic altars remain active through continual sin, sacrifices, and rituals.

How Demonic Altars Are Established

Demonic altars are erected through specific actions or events that create spiritual agreements with darkness. Some of the primary ways these altars are established include:

- Idolatry: Worshiping false gods, engaging in witchcraft, or even idolizing money, power, or relationships above God can create demonic altars.
- Ancestral Practices: Many altars are generational, established by ancestors who engaged in occult rituals, ancestral worship, or ungodly traditions. These altars persist, influencing descendants—even those unaware of their existence.
- Words and Declarations: Spoken words carry power in the spiritual realm. Curses, negative vows, and declarations made in anger or ignorance can serve as building blocks for demonic altars.
- Bloodshed: Blood sacrifices—whether through murder, abortion, or occult rituals—create and empower

demonic altars, giving the enemy strongholds in people's lives.

- Unholy Alliances: Ungodly covenants formed through false religions, occult involvement, or sinful traditions can establish demonic altars, granting access to the forces of darkness.

The Purpose of Demonic Altars

Demonic altars are built with intentional objectives designed to advance the kingdom of darkness:

- To Enforce Bondage: These altars act as spiritual prisons, trapping individuals and families in cycles of poverty, sickness, addiction, or failure.
- To Perpetuate Generational Curses: Many demonic altars hold legal rights over bloodlines, enforcing curses that pass from one generation to the next due to ancestral agreements with darkness.
- To Oppose Godly Altars: Demonic altars are established to counteract the work of God's kingdom by blocking prayers, hindering blessings, and resisting divine purposes.

- To Control Territories: Many demonic altars are territorial, influencing the spiritual climate of regions. This can manifest in widespread violence, immorality, corruption, and systemic oppression within communities.

The Power of Godly Altars: A Divine Contrast

The concept of altars is not exclusive to the enemy. Salvation results from a spiritual altar, the ultimate altar being God's throne. Christ's sacrifice on the cross established a divine altar that grants eternal redemption. No matter how powerful a demonic altar may seem, the altar of Christ's sacrifice stands above all, offering complete freedom and restoration to those who call upon His name.

Scripture Reference:
"For this reason, Christ is the mediator of a new covenant, that those who are called may receive the promised eternal inheritance."
—Hebrews 9:15

Through divine revelation and strategic prayer, demonic altars can be dismantled, and Godly altars can be established to reclaim spiritual territories and secure lasting breakthroughs.

Signs of a Demonic Altar in Your Life

Recurring negative patterns in your life, family, or community can indicate the presence of an active demonic altar. If you find yourself trapped in cycles of hardship, sickness, addiction, or failure despite your best efforts, a demonic altar may be at work.

On the other hand, Godly altars sustain blessings, breakthroughs, and divine favor. Recognizing the source of your patterns, whether positive or negative, is key to securing lasting victory

Recognizing the presence of an altar requires spiritual discernment and attentiveness to consistent patterns in your life, family, or community. Altars exert a spiritual influence that shapes destinies, manifesting as cycles of blessings or curses that persist over time. A Godly altar fuels divine favor, open doors, and breakthroughs. Conversely, if persistent struggles such as hardship, sickness, or repeated failures continue despite your best efforts, it may indicate the presence of a demonic altar sustaining those struggles. Understanding the function of altars is crucial to breaking negative cycles and securing lasting freedom.

Examples of Altars at Work

Salvation: The foundation of salvation is rooted in an altar; the ultimate altar being God's throne. This divine altar sustains the promise of redemption, ensuring that anyone who calls on the name of Jesus will be saved. The sacrifice of Christ on the cross established an eternal spiritual altar that grants believers access to salvation and eternal life.

Negative Altars: Just as Godly altars release blessings, demonic altars sustain cycles of bondage. These altars empower destructive patterns such as addictions, chronic illness, poverty, and generational curses. Their influence extends beyond individuals, impacting entire families, communities, and nations. Many people unknowingly operate under the power of such altars, as these forces gain legal rights through ancestral or personal agreements, often remaining undetected until they are intentionally broken.

One of the most apparent indicators of a demonic altar is the persistence of destructive patterns across generations. When you notice the same afflictions, failures, or tragedies repeating in a family bloodline, it is more than coincidence; it is the workings of an altar granting authorization to spiritual oppression.

1. Addictions and Immoral Behavior: Many addictions and destructive behaviors are powered by spiritual altars. Whether substance abuse, sexual perversion, or compulsive habits, these struggles often have a spiritual root. Some individuals find themselves inexplicably drawn to behaviors they detest, not realizing they are under the influence of a generational altar fueling their bondage.

2. Mystery Diseases and Infirmities: Some chronic illnesses and hereditary conditions persist due to genetics and the power of altars operating in a bloodline. While medical science offers explanations and treatments, higher spiritual intelligence reveals that certain afflictions remain because of spiritual legalities. Patterns of sickness, where a father, mother, siblings, and extended family suffer the same ailments, often indicate the presence of a sustaining altar.

3. Mental Health Struggles: Depression, anxiety, and other mental afflictions can sometimes be tied to altars. In *Matthew 8:28-34,* Jesus encountered the demon-possessed men in the region of the Gadarenes, whose suffering was not merely psychological but the result of a spiritual stronghold. While counseling and therapy are valuable, some struggles persist because they are empowered by an altar that must be dismantled.

28 When he arrived at the other side in the region of the Gadarenes,[a] two demon-possessed men coming from the tombs met him. They were so violent that no one could pass that way. 29 "What do you want with us, Son of God?" they shouted. "Have you come here to torture us before the appointed time?"

30 Some distance from them a large herd of pigs was feeding. 31 The demons begged Jesus, "If you drive us out, send us into the herd of pigs."

32 He said to them, "Go!" So they came out and went into the pigs, and the whole herd rushed down the steep bank into the lake and died in the water. 33 Those tending the pigs ran off, went into the town and reported all this, including what had happened to the demon-possessed men. 34 Then the whole town went out to meet Jesus. And when they saw him, they pleaded with him to leave their region.

—Matthew 8:28-34

4. Witchcraft and Idolatry: Altars can sustain witchcraft, idolatry, and ancestral covenants, continually pulling individuals back to ungodly foundations—even when they desire freedom. Many sincere believers struggle to fully break free from generational idolatry because the altar still speaks over their lives. Whether consciously or unconsciously, the altar remains active unless intentionally dismantled.

5. Stagnation and Delays: If you repeatedly come close to success but never entirely break through, an altar may be blocking your progress. Near-success syndrome—starting strong but never finishing, encountering sudden obstacles at the edge of breakthrough—is often a sign of an altar at work. Many individuals launch multiple businesses, ministries, or ventures, but none seem to last. This cycle is not random; it directly results from an altar resisting advancement.

6. Barrenness and Short-Lived Blessings: Some people experience great opportunities, only to see them vanish quickly. They receive financial blessings, promotions, or breakthroughs, yet shortly after, everything collapses. A common sign of an altar is the fear of joy, when someone hesitates to celebrate their success because they expect something to go wrong. This pattern is spiritual sabotage caused by an altar undermining lasting prosperity.

7. Spiritual Hindrance in Ministry and Families: Even churches, ministries, and families can unknowingly be affected by altars. These altars don't always result from personal sin but may stem from generational agreements or territorial strongholds. Such altars can influence a church's growth, a family's spiritual climate, or a leader's ability to fulfill their divine calling. Without spiritual intelligence, these hidden altars continue to exert influence behind the scenes.

Unlocking and Dismantling Demonic Altars

Breaking free from demonic altars requires intentional spiritual engagement. Here are the key steps to dismantling them:

1. Knowledge Is Power: The first step is recognizing the presence of an altar. Spiritual ignorance allows the enemy to operate freely. *Scripture Reference:*

"My people are destroyed for lack of knowledge" —**Hosea 4:6**

2. Repentance and Renunciation: Confess and renounce any personal or generational agreements with darkness that have empowered the altar. Repentance nullifies the altar's legal claim.

3. Engage in Spiritual Warfare: Use targeted prayers and fasting to break the power of the altar. Declare the blood of Jesus over your life and destroy any lingering spiritual contracts. *Scripture Reference: "For the weapons of our warfare are not carnal but mighty in God for pulling down strongholds" (2 Corinthians 10:4).*

4. Apply the Blood of Jesus: The blood of Jesus is the ultimate weapon against demonic altars. It severs every legal right the enemy holds and sets captives free.

5. Build Godly Altars: Replace demonic altars with altars to the Lord. Establish new worship, prayer, and consecration patterns in your life and family.

Conclusion

Demonic altars are often the hidden forces behind persistent struggles, stagnation, and oppression. You can break their influence and walk in lasting freedom by gaining knowledge and applying spiritual strategies. God has empowered you to dismantle every altar standing against your destiny. Victory is not only possible—it is your inheritance.

Everything that is not of God and everything powered by an altar—after this book, we will scatter it once and for all.

Closing Prayer

Father, in the mighty name of Jesus Christ, I thank You for exposing the hidden works of darkness and revealing the truth about demonic altars. I declare that I will no longer walk in ignorance or bondage, but in the authority and liberty You have given me.

Lord, I repent for every sin, agreement, or covenant, personal or generational, that has empowered any altar working against my life. I renounce all connections to darkness and command every altar speaking failure, sickness, poverty, delay, or destruction to be silenced by the blood of Jesus.

I plead the blood of Jesus over my life, family, and bloodline. Let every legal right the enemy has claimed be revoked now. By the authority of the name of Jesus and through the power of the Holy Spirit, I command every demonic altar to be dismantled, uprooted, and consumed by Holy Fire. Let every spiritual structure resisting my progress crumble now!

Father, establish in me and my household a godly altar, an altar of worship, prayer, holiness, and covenant with You. May Your presence dwell with me, and may Your favor follow me all the days of my life. I receive total freedom and declare that cycles of bondage are broken forever.

Thank you, Lord, for victory! Thank you for the revelation. Thank you for the power to walk in the fullness of my divine destiny.

In Jesus' mighty name, I pray.
Amen.

CHAPTER 2:
Spiritual Legalities: Understanding the Laws of Altars

Throughout history, altars have served as spiritual gateways, where humanity connects with the divine or the demonic realm. These physical or spiritual structures operate under legal principles that govern their power and effectiveness. Understanding the spiritual legalities behind altars is essential for breaking free from demonic strongholds and establishing godly dominion in your life.

One of the greatest deceptions of the enemy is convincing believers that demonic altars do not influence their lives. However, Scripture makes it clear that the spiritual realm operates on legalities. Satan leverages these legalities to build cases against God's people and enforce spiritual bondage.

In *Genesis 4:10*, after Cain killed Abel, God said, **"The voice of your brother's blood cries out to Me from the ground."**

This reveals that bloodshed establishes a legal right for spiritual entities to operate, whether for good or evil. Demonic altars often exploit unrepentant sin, ancestral iniquities, or curses to maintain their influence.

The Foundation of Spiritual Legalities

Like the natural world, the spiritual realm operates on laws and principles. In Genesis, God established divine order and rules that govern all of creation, including the spiritual world. Altars, as points of contact between realms, function within these laws. They require sacrifices, covenants, and authority to operate. These unseen legalities govern how good and evil spiritual forces gain access to people's lives. Understanding these laws is vital for anyone seeking to break free from demonic influence and secure lasting spiritual victory.

The Spiritual Courtroom: How Legalities Operate

> The Bible reveals that the spiritual realm mirrors a courtroom. In *Job 1:6-12,* we see Satan appearing before God to accuse Job. This courtroom setting shows that Satan builds legal cases against believers to enforce curses, afflictions, and spiritual bondage. Demonic altars are empowered through these legal systems, giving the enemy the right to operate in the lives of individuals, families, and even entire regions.

6 One day the angels came to present themselves before the Lord, and Satan also came with them.

7 The Lord said to Satan, "Where have you come from?"

Satan answered the Lord, "From roaming throughout the earth, going back and forth on it."

8 Then the Lord said to Satan, "Have you considered my servant Job? There is no one on earth like him; he is blameless and upright, a man who fears God and shuns evil."

9 "Does Job fear God for nothing?" Satan replied.

10 "Have you not put a hedge around him and his household and everything he has? You have blessed the work of his hands, so that his flocks and herds are spread throughout the land.

11 But now stretch out your hand and strike everything he has, and he will surely curse you to your face."

12 The Lord said to Satan, "Very well, then, everything he has is in your power, but on the man himself do not lay a finger." Then Satan went out from the presence of the Lord.

—Job 1:6-12

The courts of heaven provide a framework for addressing spiritual legalities. Picture a courtroom where God is the Judge, Jesus is your Advocate, and Satan is the Accuser *(Revelation 12:10)*

10 Then I heard a loud voice in heaven say:

"Now have come the salvation and the power
and the kingdom of our God,
and the authority of his Messiah.
For the accuser of our brothers and sisters,
who accuses them before our God day and night,
has been hurled down.

- **Presenting Your Case:** When you approach God in prayer, present your case based on the finished work of Christ. Declare that Jesus' blood has paid the price for your freedom, making any demonic claims over your life invalid.

- **Repenting of Iniquity:** Repentance removes the legal grounds for the enemy's accusations. Confess generational sins, asking for God's forgiveness and cleansing.

- **Enforcing the Verdict:** Once God issues a verdict of freedom, enforce it through declarations and spiritual warfare. Command every demonic spirit tied to old altars to leave in Jesus' name.

Key Legal Principles That Govern Altars

To understand how demonic altars manipulate lives, we must examine several key legal principles:

- **Altars and Time:** Altars are not limited by time. Their spiritual impact can extend across generations, influencing descendants long after the original person who erected them has passed. For instance, Abraham's altar became a place of encounter for his descendants, including Jacob. The presence and power of an altar remain even when its physical creator is no longer present.

- **The Law of Agreement:** Amos 3:3 asks, *"Can two walk together unless they are agreed?"*

    Agreement is a powerful spiritual principle that empowers both Godly and Ungodly forces. When a person willingly or unknowingly engages in sin, occult practices, or ungodly covenants, they agree with the kingdom of darkness. This agreement empowers demonic altars to gain legal access.

- **The Law of Blood:** Blood sacrifices are among the most potent legal transactions in the spiritual realm. In *Genesis 4:10,* Abel's blood cried out from the ground, demonstrating that blood carries a voice in the spirit. Occult rituals, sacrifices, or even acts of violence can establish demonic altars that claim authority over individuals or families.

- **The Law of Covenants:** A covenant is a binding spiritual contract. When ungodly covenants are formed—whether through family traditions, generational practices, or deliberate involvement in the occult—demonic altars are empowered to enforce oppression until those covenants are broken. *Joshua 9:15-20* shows how Israel mistakenly made a covenant with the Gibeonites. Even though it was formed deceitfully, it remained legally binding, proving that covenants must be consciously addressed and revoked.

15 Then Joshua made a treaty of peace with them to let them live, and the leaders of the assembly ratified it by oath.

16 Three days after they made the treaty with the Gibeonites, the Israelites heard that they were neighbors, living near them.

17 So the Israelites set out and on the third day came to their cities: Gibeon, Kephirah, Beeroth, and Kiriath Jearim.

18 But the Israelites did not attack them, because the leaders of the assembly had sworn an oath to them by the Lord, the God of Israel. The whole assembly grumbled against the leaders,

19 but all the leaders answered, "We have given them our oath by the Lord, the God of Israel, and we cannot touch them now."

20 This is what we will do to them: We will let them live, so that God's wrath will not fall on us for breaking the oath we swore to them.

—Joshua 9:15-20

- **The Law of Words:** Words can establish or dismantle spiritual agreements. ***Proverbs 18:21*** declares, ***"Death and life are in the power of the tongue."***

Negative declarations, curses spoken by those in authority, or self-sabotaging words can fuel demonic altars and keep individuals bound.

- **The Law of Inheritance:** Spiritual legalities can extend across bloodlines. In Exodus 20:5, God warns that the fathers' sins can visit subsequent generations. This principle reveals how demonic altars linked to ancestors may continue to afflict descendants unless the curse is broken.

- **Authority and Ownership:** An altar is only as powerful as the spiritual authority behind it. When an altar is erected, it signifies ownership and dominion. In the Old Testament, altars were built to claim land for God *(Genesis 12:7).* Conversely, demonic altars claim territories and individuals for darkness. Authority is transferred through covenants. For example, generational curses often stem from ancestral covenants made at demonic altars. These legalities permit demonic forces to operate until the covenant is broken through the blood of Jesus.

Covenants and Agreements

Altars are places where covenants are established. Covenants are binding agreements in the spiritual realm, giving legal rights to spiritual entities. For example, God's covenant with Abraham was sealed at an altar *(Genesis 15:9-18).*

9 So the Lord said to him, "Bring me a heifer, a goat, and a ram, each three years old, along with a dove and a young pigeon."

10 Abram brought all these to him, cut them in two and arranged the halves opposite each other; the birds, however, he did not cut in half.

11 Then birds of prey came down on the carcasses, but Abram drove them away.

12 As the sun was setting, Abram fell into a deep sleep, and a thick and dreadful darkness came over him.

13 Then the Lord said to him, "Know for certain that for four hundred years your descendants will be strangers in a country not their own and that they will be enslaved and mistreated there.

14 But I will punish the nation they serve as slaves, and afterward, they will come out with great possessions.

15 You, however, will go to your ancestors in peace and be buried at a good old age.

16 In the fourth generation, your descendants will come back here, for the sin of the Amorites has not yet reached its full measure."

17 When the sun had set and darkness had fallen, a smoking firepot with a blazing torch appeared and passed between the pieces.

18 On that day the Lord made a covenant with Abram

and said, "To your descendants, I give this land, from the Wadi of Egypt to the great river, the Euphrates."

Demonic altars operate on the same principle. If someone in your bloodline made a pact with a demonic entity, that agreement creates a legal right for oppression until it is renounced and broken.

Sacrifice: The Currency of Altars

Every altar requires a sacrifice. In the Bible, Godly altars demanded offerings such as lambs, doves, or incense **(Exodus 30:7-10)**. These sacrifices invited God's presence and favor.

Exodus 30:7-10 (NIV)
7 "Aaron must burn fragrant incense on the altar every morning when he tends the lamps.
8 He must burn incense again when he lights the lamps at twilight so incense will burn regularly before the Lord for the generations to come.
9 Do not offer on this altar any other incense or any burnt offering or grain offering, and do not pour a drink offering on it.
10 Once a year Aaron shall make atonement on its horns. This annual atonement must be made with the blood of the atoning sin offering for the generations to come. It is most holy to the Lord."

At demonic altars, sacrifices often involve blood, rituals, or sinful acts. These sacrifices empower demonic forces to carry out their agenda. Without sacrifice, an altar loses its power and influence.

Practical Steps to Understanding and Applying Spiritual Legalities

- **Study Scripture:** Familiarize yourself with stories of altars in the Bible and how they were used to establish covenants, claim territory, and invoke God's presence.

- **Engage in Deliverance:** Seek deliverance ministry if you suspect demonic altars are affecting your life. A trained minister can guide you through renouncing covenants and breaking curses.

- **Build a Lifestyle of Worship:** Worship and prayer create a godly altar. Invite the Holy Spirit to dwell with you and establish His authority over every area of your life.

Conclusion

Understanding the laws of altars equips you to dismantle demonic strongholds and build Godly altars that invite God's power and presence. Spiritual legalities are not to be feared but understood and applied through the authority of Jesus Christ. You can walk in freedom, victory, and divine purpose by aligning with God's laws. Spiritual legalities are real, and demonic altars thrive when believers are unaware of these unseen contracts. Understanding and applying God's Word can overturn demonic legal claims, break free from generational strongholds, and secure lasting victory. Remember, God has given you the authority to challenge and defeat every altar that opposes your destiny.

Closing Prayer

Father, in Jesus' name, I thank You for revealing spiritual legalities and helping me understand the laws that govern the realm of the Spirit. I acknowledge Your sovereignty over all creation and the authority You have given me through the blood of Jesus Christ.

Lord, I ask for Your grace to discern and break every demonic stronghold and altar that has held me captive. I renounce every ungodly covenant, agreement, and ritual that has been established in my life or bloodline. I command every spirit of oppression, bondage, and darkness to leave in the mighty name of Jesus.

Father, I stand firm in the authority of Your Word, knowing that no weapon formed against me shall prosper. I declare that

I am free from the influence of any demonic altar, and I claim the victory of the Cross over my life. I invite Your Holy Spirit to establish godly altars in my heart and offer my life as a living sacrifice, holy and pleasing to You.

Lord, empower me to walk in spiritual victory, to enforce the verdicts of freedom, and to establish Your kingdom in every area of my life. I thank You for the wisdom and strength to continue in Your truth, and I trust that You are with me every step of the way.

In Jesus' name, I pray. Amen.

CHAPTER 3:
How Demonic Altars Are Built to Bind You

Demonic altars are not built by accident. They are intentionally constructed through deliberate actions, spiritual agreements, and often, generational iniquities. Understanding how these altars are formed is crucial for dismantling their influence and reclaiming your spiritual freedom.

The Foundation of Demonic Altars

A demonic altar is a point of contact between the spiritual and natural realms. While Godly altars invite the presence and power of God, demonic altars draw dark forces that enforce bondage, sickness, and destruction. Legal rights often fortify these altars, allowing the enemy to operate in a person's life or family.

The Blueprint of a Demonic Altar

- **Sin and Iniquity as the Foundation**

  Sin is the foundational element upon which demonic altars are built. When individuals or families repeatedly engage in sinful behavior, they create an environment conducive to demonic activity. Iniquity, which is sin passed down through generations, strengthens these altars. For example, patterns of addiction, abuse, or idolatry in a family line often reveal an altar established by past generations.

Scripture Reference:

"If I regard iniquity in my heart, the Lord will not hear me"

—**Psalm 66:1**

- **Covenants and Agreements**

  Demonic altars are frequently established through covenants, whether knowingly or unknowingly. These covenants may involve blood oaths, sacrifices, or rituals performed by ancestors. Agreements made through witchcraft, occult practices, or false religions also contribute to the formation of these altars. Even seemingly innocent actions, like participating in cultural rituals, can bind individuals to demonic covenants if those rituals are rooted in idolatry.

- **Sacrifices and Offerings**

    Sacrifices are the currency of spiritual altars. At demonic altars, sacrifices may include blood (animal or human), time, money, or sinful acts like sexual immorality.

    Each sacrifice strengthens the altar and grants demonic entities greater access and authority to operate.

- **Words and Declarations**

    Words carry immense power in the spiritual realm. Negative declarations, curses, or vows made by individuals or spoken over them can fuel demonic altars. For example, a parent declaring, "You'll never amount to anything," can create a spiritual agreement that binds a child to failure.

    Scripture Reference:

    "Death and life are in the power of the tongue."

    —Proverbs 18:21

- **Objects and Symbols**

    Physical objects—such as charms, idols, or cursed

items—can be points of contact for demonic altars.

These objects often symbolize dedication to demonic forces, allowing evil spirits to maintain a foothold in a person's life or home.

How Demonic Altars Bind You

Once a demonic altar is established, it begins to influence various key areas of your life:

- **Spiritual Bondage**
  Demonic altars create spiritual contracts that bind individuals to cycles of sin, poverty, sickness, or oppression. These cycles persist until the altar is dismantled through deliverance. For example, an altar built on sexual immorality may manifest as generational patterns of infidelity, divorce, or promiscuity.

- **Mental and Emotional Bondage**
  Altars often target the mind and emotions, sowing seeds of fear, anxiety, depression, and confusion. Thoughts of self-doubt, worthlessness, and confusion are reinforced by the spiritual strongholds established at these altars. Anxiety, depression, or uncontrollable anger can stem from spiritual bondage rooted in these altars.

- **Physical Bondage**

   Some demonic altars manifest as physical illnesses or infirmities. These conditions may resist medical treatment because their root cause is spiritual.

   Generational patterns of diseases, such as cancer, heart disease, or infertility, often point to demonic altars in the bloodline.

- **Financial Bondage**

   Demonic altars can block financial breakthroughs and keep individuals stuck in cycles of debt, poverty, or lack. These altars are often rooted in covenants involving greed, theft, or dishonesty.

- **Territorial Bondage**

   Altars can also bind entire regions or communities, giving demonic forces control over the spiritual atmosphere.

   For example, areas plagued by violence, poverty, or idolatry may be under the influence of territorial altars.

How Demonic Altars Are Maintained

- **Repetition of Sin**

   Continuous sin feeds the altar and keeps it active. Without repentance, the altar remains a stronghold.

Scripture Reference: "The wages of sin is death" (Romans 6:23).

- **Generational Agreements**

  Family members who continue in the same sins or rituals unknowingly renew the covenants tied to demonic altars.

- **Unbroken Curses**

  Curses spoken over individuals or families can keep altars alive. These curses must be identified and broken through prayer and fasting.

- **Ignorance and Passivity**

  Lack of knowledge about spiritual warfare allows demonic altars to remain unchallenged. The enemy thrives on ignorance.

  Scripture Reference:

  "My people are destroyed for lack of knowledge" —Hosea 4:6.

Understanding the Roots of Demonic Altars

Demonic altars don't just appear—they are established through specific actions, agreements, and covenants. Many of these altars are deeply rooted in your bloodline, tracing back to previous generations' sins, practices, and agreements. To fully understand their influence, we must examine their origins (Spiritual mapping):

- **Generational Sins and Iniquities**
  Scripture tells us that the sins of the fathers can affect multiple generations *(Exodus 20:5)*. Practices such as idolatry, witchcraft, and ungodly rituals create spiritual footholds for demonic altars in family lines.
  These generational altars often manifest as recurring patterns of poverty, sickness, addiction, or marital issues.

- **Unbroken Covenants**
  Covenants made by ancestors with demonic forces, whether through rituals, vows, or secret societies, serve as legal agreements in the spiritual realm. Until these covenants are broken, the altars remain active.

- **Trauma and Bloodshed**
  Events involving bloodshed, such as violence, abuse, or untimely deaths, provide a spiritual foundation for

demonic altars. The enemy uses these events as gateways to establish his influence.

- **Personal Sins and Agreements**
    Personal actions, such as engaging in occult practices, sexual immorality, or idolatry, can either establish new altars or strengthen existing ones. These actions give the enemy legal access to operate in your life.

Conclusion

Demonic altars are built to enslave, but the power of Jesus Christ is more significant than any altar of darkness. By understanding how these altars are constructed and maintained, you can take the necessary steps to dismantle them and walk in total freedom. God has given you the authority to break every chain and destroy every stronghold, allowing His light to shine in every area of your life.

Closing Prayer:

Father, in the name of Jesus, I thank You for the revelation You've given me about the demonic altars that have sought to bind me and my family. I thank You for the power of Your truth that breaks every stronghold, dismantles every altar, and brings freedom into every area of my life.

Lord, I now lay before You every altar of darkness that has operated in my bloodline, mind, body, and finances. I renounce every covenant, agreement, and sinful practice that has given the enemy legal access to my life. I declare that the power of Your blood now destroys every demonic altar, and every legal claim of the enemy is made null and void.

I thank You, Father, for the spiritual authority You've given me in Christ Jesus. I speak to every area of my life bound by these altars and declare freedom in Jesus' name. I receive your victory, peace, and deliverance over every chain that has held me captive.

Holy Spirit, I invite You to move in every area of my life. Come and fill the spaces once occupied by darkness, and establish Your divine order. I thank you for the restoration that is taking place, the freedom I walk in today, and the mighty work you are doing in me.

Thank you, Lord, for setting me free. I receive Your truth, Your freedom, and Your victory today. In Jesus' name, I pray. Amen.

Part 2

Breaking The Chains of Darkness

CHAPTER 4:

Breaking Free- Identifying Demonic Altar in your life and your blood line

Breaking free from demonic altars is not a **one-time event** but an ongoing journey of spiritual growth, vigilance, and intentional action. As you dismantle these altars and sever their ties to your life, you'll experience the freedom, peace, and blessings God intended for you.

Remember, the authority to break free lies in Jesus Christ. His sacrifice on the cross nullified every covenant with the enemy and destroyed the power of every demonic altar. By standing in His authority, you can live a life of unshakable victory, walking boldly in God's promises.

Recognizing the presence of demonic altars in your life or family is the first critical step toward achieving spiritual freedom. These altars often operate invisibly, but their influence manifests in persistent struggles, negative cycles, and unexplainable resistance to progress. You can strategically break free and walk in lasting victory by identifying their presence.

Signs of a Demonic Altar in Operation

Demonic altars leave distinct spiritual footprints; identifying them is key to breaking free. Here are some common indicators that a demonic altar may be influencing your life or family:

- **Recurring Patterns of Failure**
    Cycles of financial hardship, broken relationships, or chronic illnesses may point to a spiritual stronghold rooted in an altar. If you find yourself stuck in failure patterns despite your best efforts, it may be time to examine the spiritual roots.

- **Family Bondage**
    Generational struggles, such as addictions, premature deaths, or constant misfortune, may indicate an ancestral altar at work. These altars operate across bloodlines, passing down curses or strongholds unless broken.

- **Unexplainable Oppression**
    Sudden emotional heaviness, constant fear, disturbing dreams, or feelings of being overwhelmed are often

signs of demonic manipulation. If you experience a sense of oppression that doesn't seem to have a logical explanation, it may be tied to an altar.

- **Repeated Blockages and Delays**
  If you consistently face obstacles when trying to advance in life, whether in ministry, career, or personal endeavors, this could be a sign of an altar resisting your progress. Altars often block success and hold you back from your God-given potential.

- **Negative Words and Declarations**
  Curses, word curses, or negative declarations spoken over you, especially by those in authority, may empower a demonic altar. Words have power, and negative declarations can give the enemy legal ground in your life.

How Demonic Altars Gain Access

Demonic altars gain control through specific spiritual entry points. Understanding these access points is crucial in uncovering their origin and breaking their power:

- **Generational Curses**
  Sins, oaths, or covenants established by ancestors can empower an altar to influence entire family lines.

Fathers' sins can be visited upon the children (Exodus 20:5), and these generational curses can perpetuate cycles of defeat.

5 You shall not bow down to them or worship them; for I, the Lord your God, am a jealous God, punishing the children for the sin of the parents to the third and fourth generation of those who hate me,

—Exodus 20:5

- **Personal Sin and Disobedience**

    Ongoing sin, rebellion, or unforgiveness opens doors for demonic influence. Any unrepentant sin gives the enemy legal access to operate. The enemy's foothold often begins with personal disobedience or unchecked iniquity.

- **Objects and Materials**

    Occult objects, cursed items, or symbols linked to false religions can unknowingly empower demonic altars. Items like charms, idols, or even certain heirlooms can serve as points of contact for the enemy, perpetuating the power of demonic altars.

Tools for Identifying Demonic Altars

Breaking free requires discernment and spiritual insight. Here are some practical tools to help you identify demonic altars in your life:

1. **Prayer and Revelation from the Holy Spirit**
   Ask God to reveal hidden altars affecting your life. Jeremiah 33:3 says,

   "Call to Me, and I will answer you, and show you great and mighty things you do not know." —Jeremiah 33:3

   The Holy Spirit will guide you to uncover what is hidden.

2. **Examining Your Family History (Spiritual Mapping)**
   Look for recurring patterns of sin, hardship, or spiritual issues in your family line. These patterns often reveal the presence of generational altars. Take time to reflect on past family struggles, addictions, early deaths, broken relationships, and discern their spiritual origin.

3. **Analyzing Your Life Patterns**
   Reflect on areas of repeated struggle, failure, or resistance. These patterns can point to specific altars

influencing your life. If you experience constant setbacks or difficulty breaking free from negative cycles, you may be dealing with the effects of demonic altars.

4. **Paying Attention to Dreams and Visions**

   God often uses dreams to reveal spiritual realities. Dreams of being tied, pursued, or engaged in rituals can signify the presence of demonic altars. Pay attention to dreams where you feel trapped, chased, or involved in strange rituals; these are often spiritual signals.

5. **Seeking Prophetic Insight**

   A trusted prophetic voice can clarify and confirm the altars' presence and origins. Prophets can often discern hidden spiritual structures and reveal the roots of spiritual strongholds in your life.

Steps to Break Free from Demonic Altars

Once you've identified the altars in your life, it's time to take action. Breaking free involves targeted spiritual warfare and the application of biblical principles:

Remember, deliverance is the children's bread and our inheritance as believers. The keyword here is believers. Before breaking demonic altars or experiencing true freedom, you must start with salvation.

If you have not yet accepted Jesus as your Lord and Savior, I invite you to take this crucial first step. Without Jesus, you have no legal grounds to move forward in your deliverance. You have no claims that you can stand on or present in the courtroom of heaven. Salvation is the key to accessing your inheritance in Christ and beginning the journey of freedom.

If you are ready to receive salvation and walk in the victory Christ has already secured for you, simply pray this prayer:

Prayer of Salvation:

Lord Jesus, I come to You today acknowledging that I am a sinner in need of Your grace and forgiveness. I believe You died for my sins and God raised You from the dead. I ask You to come into my heart, to be my Lord and Savior, and to make me a new creation in You. I surrender my life to You and commit to following You from now on. Thank you for your love, your sacrifice, and the gift of eternal life. In Jesus' name, Amen.

You are now saved if you prayed that prayer with all your heart. The first step toward your deliverance has been made, and the doors to your freedom are now open. From this point forward, you have legal access to the power of Jesus and His victory over the enemy.

Now, as a child of God, you can begin to break every

stronghold and walk in the freedom that is yours by inheritance in Christ.

- **Repentance and Renunciation**

    Repent of any personal or ancestral sins that contributed to the establishment of the altar. Confess and renounce any covenants, vows, or agreements made with the kingdom of darkness. Repentance is the key to breaking the enemy's legal hold.

- **Breaking Generational Curses**

    Declare that the power of generational curses is broken through the blood of Jesus. Galatians 3:13 reminds us that Christ has redeemed us from the law's curse so that we can walk in freedom.

- **Targeted Prayers and Declarations**

    Pray fervently to dismantle the altar and nullify its influence. Use Scriptures like 2 Corinthians 10:4-5, which says,

"The weapons of our warfare are not carnal but mighty in God for pulling down strongholds."

Your prayers must be specific and direct, addressing the altars and their influence.

- **Destroying Legal Rights**

  Speak directly to the altar, declaring it has no more legal right to operate in your life. Apply the blood of Jesus to revoke its power. By standing on the authority of the Word, you can cancel every demonic claim.

- **Fasting and Spiritual Warfare**

  Fasting is a powerful tool for breaking spiritual strongholds. Combine fasting with targeted prayers for maximum effectiveness. Jesus said,

  "This kind can come out by nothing but prayer and fasting" —Mark 9:29

- **Establishing Godly Altars**

  Replace the demonic altar with a godly altar. Dedicate your life, home, and family to God through prayer, worship, and obedience. As you tear down the altars of darkness, build altars of light that honor and invite God's presence into your life.

- **Maintaining Your Deliverance**

  Walk in obedience and stay connected to God through prayer and His Word. Surround yourself with a community of believers who can support and encourage you in your journey. Stay vigilant and strengthen your relationship with God to guard against future attacks.

Conclusion

Breaking free from demonic altars is a journey that requires persistence, faith, and spiritual insight. By identifying their presence, renouncing their power, and applying the blood of Jesus, you will walk in the victory and freedom that God has destined for you. Remember, your authority in Christ is more significant than any altar erected to bind you. Stand firm in that truth and claim your freedom in Christ Jesus.

Closing Prayer:

Father, in the name of Jesus, I thank You for the revelation You've provided through this chapter. I thank you for exposing the hidden altars that have bound me and my family, and I declare that I am now equipped with the knowledge and authority to break free from their influence.

Lord, I repent for any sin, covenant, or agreement that has opened the door for demonic altars to operate in my life or bloodline. I ask for your forgiveness and cleansing and renounce every generational curse, vow, and demonic stronghold. I apply the blood of Jesus to every legal claim that the enemy has had over me and my family.

By Your power, I break every chain, every cycle of failure, and every spirit of oppression tied to these altars. I declare that no altar of darkness will stand in my life any longer. In the name of Jesus, I sever every legal tie to these altars and decree that they are dismantled, destroyed, and powerless.

Holy Spirit, I invite You to establish Your presence and authority in my life. Build within me a godly altar of worship, prayer, and obedience that honors You in every area. I dedicate my life, home, and family to You, Lord.

Thank you for the freedom, victory, and peace that I now walk in. I choose to walk in the fullness of the authority You've given me, standing firm in the finished work of Jesus Christ. I receive Your peace, Your healing, and Your restoration today.

In Jesus' mighty name, I pray. Amen.

CHAPTER 5:
The Battle Plan: Spiritual Warfare and the Power of Prayer

The journey to spiritual freedom is not passive; it requires intentional action, strategic warfare, and unwavering faith in God's power. Spiritual warfare is the believer's battle against the forces of darkness, and prayer is the most potent weapon in this fight. To dismantle demonic altars and reclaim your spiritual inheritance, you need a clear battle plan rooted in biblical principles and executed with the authority of Christ.

Understanding Spiritual Warfare

Spiritual warfare is the ongoing conflict between the kingdom of God and the forces of darkness. It's not a battle fought with physical weapons but with spiritual authority, discernment, and the power of prayer. As **Ephesians 6:12** reminds us:

"For we do not wrestle against flesh and blood, but against principalities, against powers, against the rulers of the darkness of this age, against spiritual hosts of wickedness in the heavenly places."

The enemy's ultimate goal is to steal, kill, and destroy **(John 10:10)**. Demonic altars are one of his primary tools for enforcing his destructive plans. However, we can dismantle these altars and destroy the enemy's works through Christ.

The Role of Prayer in Spiritual Warfare

Prayer is not just a conversation with God but a weapon of mass destruction in the spiritual realm. When you pray with faith and authority, you activate heaven's power to overturn demonic schemes. As **James 5:16** declares,

"The effective, fervent prayer of a righteous man avails much."

Through prayer, you:

- **Access Divine Authority**: Prayer allows you to operate in the authority of Christ, who has already defeated the enemy **(Luke 10:19)**.

I have given you the authority to trample on snakes and scorpions and to overcome all the power of the enemy; nothing will harm you.

- **Pull Down Strongholds:** Prayer dismantles spiritual strongholds and nullifies the power of demonic altars **(2 Corinthians 10:4)**.

4 The weapons we fight with are not the weapons of the world. On the contrary, they have divine power to demolish strongholds.

- **Release Angelic Assistance**: Your prayers activate angels to war on your behalf **(Daniel 10:12-13)**.

Then he continued, "Do not be afraid, Daniel. Since the first day that you set your mind to gain understanding and to humble yourself before your God, your words were heard, and I have come in response to them. 13 But the prince of the Persian kingdom resisted me twenty-one days. Then Michael, one of the chief princes, came to help me, because I was detained there with the king of Persia.

- **Establish God's Will**: Prayer aligns your life with God's purposes and brings His kingdom to earth **(Matthew 6:10)**

"Your kingdom come, your will be done, on earth as it is in heaven".

The Battle Plan:
Steps to Engaging in Spiritual Warfare

Following a strategic plan to engage in spiritual warfare is essential. Here's how to do it:

1. Recognize the Enemy

Before entering the battlefield, you must first identify your enemy. The enemy operates in deception, often hiding behind life's circumstances. Discern the spiritual root of your struggles through prayer and revelation from the Holy Spirit. Understanding the nature of the battle equips you for victory.

2. Clothe Yourself in Spiritual Armor

Ephesians 6:10-18 outlines the whole armor of God, which equips you for battle:

- **The Belt of Truth:** Stand firm in God's truth to counter the enemy's lies.

- **The Breastplate of Righteousness:** Live a life of holiness and integrity.

- **The Shield of Faith:** Use faith to extinguish the enemy's fiery darts of doubt and fear.

- **The Helmet of Salvation:** Guard your mind with the assurance of your salvation.

- **The Sword of the Spirit:** Wield the Word of God as a weapon against the enemy.

- **The Shoes of Peace:** Walk confidently in the peace that comes from knowing God is with you.

3. Engage in Strategic Prayer

Use targeted prayers to dismantle demonic altars and sever their influence in your life. These prayers should be:

- **Specific**: Address the altar by name and the areas of your life it affects.

- **Scripture-Based**: Declare God's Word, which is sharper than any two-edged sword (Hebrews 4:12)

- **Authoritative:** Command the altar to be destroyed in the name of Jesus.

Example Prayer:

"In the name of Jesus, I dismantle every demonic altar operating in my life and bloodline. I revoke every covenant and nullify every sacrifice made at these altars. By the power of the blood of Jesus, I declare that these altars have no authority over me."

4. Fast for Breakthrough

Fasting is a powerful tool for spiritual warfare. It intensifies your prayers and weakens the hold of the enemy. **Isaiah 58:6** says,

"Is this not the fast that I have chosen: to loose the bonds of wickedness, to undo the heavy burdens, to let the oppressed go free, and that you break every yoke?"

Types of Fasts: **(Always pray and ask God what fast you should enter. You must consult God because every battle is not fought with the same weapons.)**

- **Partial Fast:** Fasting certain meals or types of food.

- **Complete Fast:** Abstaining from all food for a designated period.

- **Daniel Fast**: Consuming only fruits, vegetables, and water. (Daniel lived a lifestyle of fasting)

5. Declare God's Word

Speak the Word of God over your situation daily. Declarations of Scripture build your faith and establish God's promises in your life.

Example Declarations:

- *"No weapon formed against me shall prosper"* **(Isaiah 54:17).**

- ***"I have been given authority to trample on serpents and scorpions, and over all the power of the enemy"*** **—Luke 10:19**

- *"Whom the Son sets free is free indeed"* —John 8:36

6. Engage in Worship

Worship is a weapon of warfare that confuses the enemy and establishes God's presence. In **2 Chronicles 20,** Jehoshaphat sent worshippers ahead of his army, and God delivered them from their enemies.

7. Call on Angelic Assistance

Angels are ministering spirits sent to aid believers **(Hebrews 1:14)**. Ask God to release His angels to fight on your behalf and guard you during battle.

8. Seal Your Victory with the Blood of Jesus

The blood of Jesus is the ultimate weapon against demonic forces. Revelation 12:11 says,

"They overcame him by the blood of the Lamb and by the word of their testimony."

Plead the blood of Jesus over your life, family, and circumstances.

Sustaining Victory Through Daily Discipline

Spiritual warfare is not a one-time event but an ongoing battle. To sustain your victory:

- Maintain a consistent prayer life.
- Stay rooted in God's Word.
- Surround yourself with a community of believers who can support you in prayer.

- Avoid actions or environments that could reopen spiritual doors to the enemy.

The Power of Prayer in Action

Throughout Scripture, we see the power of prayer at work:

- Elijah prayed, and fire came down from heaven to consume the altar **(1 Kings 18:38)**

   38 Then the fire of the LORD fell and burned up the sacrifice, the wood, the stones and the soil, and also licked up the water in the trench.

- Daniel's prayers led to angelic intervention and revelations of God's plans **(Daniel 10:12-13).**

   12 Then he continued, "Do not be afraid, Daniel. Since the first day that you set your mind to gain understanding and to humble yourself before your God, your words were heard, and I have come in response to them. 13 But the prince of the Persian kingdom resisted me twenty-one days. Then Michael, one of the chief princes, came to help me, because I was detained there with the king of Persia.

- Paul and Silas prayed and sang hymns in prison, and God caused an earthquake to set them free **(Acts 16:25-26)**.

25 About midnight Paul and Silas were praying and singing hymns to God, and the other prisoners were listening to them. 26 Suddenly there was such a violent earthquake that the foundations of the prison were shaken. At once all the prison doors flew open, and everyone's chains came loose.

These examples remind us that prayer is a force that moves heaven and earth. When combined with faith, obedience, and spiritual authority, it dismantles demonic altars, breaks chains, and ushers in freedom.

You Are Equipped for Victory

As a child of God, you are not fighting for victory; you are fighting from victory. Jesus has already defeated the enemy on your behalf **(Colossians 2:15)**.

15 And having disarmed the powers and authorities, he made a public spectacle of them, triumphing over them by the cross.

By following this battle plan and wielding the power of prayer, you will walk in the freedom and authority that Christ has secured for you.

This chapter equips you with actionable strategies for engaging in spiritual warfare, using the power of prayer to dismantle demonic altars, and reclaiming your spiritual inheritance. It serves as a blueprint for victory, empowering you to confront the forces of darkness and walk boldly in your God-given authority.

Conclusion

Victory in spiritual warfare is secured through steadfast prayer, obedience, and reliance on God's Word. As you engage in this divine battle plan, remember that Jesus Christ has already won. You will walk in freedom and spiritual triumph by aligning yourself with His authority and power.

Closing Prayer

Father, in Jesus' name, I thank You for the powerful truths You have revealed in this chapter. I stand in awe of Your Word and the authority You have given me as a believer in Christ. I am fully equipped to engage in spiritual warfare and walk in the victory you have already secured for me.

Lord, I come before You in humility, asking for Your strength and guidance as I battle against the forces of darkness. I put on the whole armor of God and stand firm in Your truth, righteousness, peace, faith, salvation, and the Word of God. I declare that no weapon formed against me shall prosper, and the power of prayer is tearing down every stronghold.

I thank You, Father, for the weapon of prayer, for the ability to command and declare in Jesus' name, and for the victory that is mine through Your finished work on the Cross. I ask Your Holy Spirit to continually guide me in strategic prayer and empower my spiritual discernment.

I also thank you for the gift of fasting and the breakthrough that comes through pressing in and seeking Your face. As I apply the principles of spiritual warfare, I declare that every demonic altar in my life is being dismantled, and I am walking in the freedom Christ has purchased for me.

Lord, I ask that You continue to reveal the hidden altars that need to be destroyed and give me the courage to take action against them. May Your fire fall upon every stronghold, and may Your presence fill every area of my life with peace, power, and victory.

I seal this time of prayer with the blood of Jesus, knowing that I have already overcome through His sacrifice. I walk in the victory that You have promised, and I declare that I will continue to stand firm, fully armored, and ready for battle, knowing that You are with me every step.

In Jesus' mighty name, I pray. Amen.

CHAPTER 6:
Destroying Demonic Altars: Step-by-Step Spiritual Victory

Demonic altars are not just spiritual structures; they are deeply entrenched strongholds designed to enforce curses, limit your destiny, and perpetuate evil patterns in your life and bloodline. These altars must be confronted and destroyed to walk in complete deliverance and freedom. This chapter will guide you through a detailed, step-by-step process for demolishing demonic altars and claiming your spiritual victory in Christ.

Step 1: Spiritual Preparation

Spiritual preparation is essential before you begin praying and breaking altars. Deliverance is a process that requires a fully committed and spiritually grounded approach. When you approach this task, you are engaging in a battle against unseen forces. Therefore, you must be fully equipped spiritually to contend with these forces.

- **Repentance and Confession:** First, ask God to reveal any hidden sins, ungodly covenants, or open doors that may have allowed the enemy access to your life. Sometimes, areas of sin, such as unforgiveness or unrepentant trauma, may be deeply hidden in your subconscious. Pray for the Holy Spirit to reveal any strongholds and areas of disobedience. Confession and repentance cleanse the soul and close the door that the enemy might have been using.

Scripture Reference: *"If we confess our sins, He is faithful and just to forgive us our sins and to cleanse us from all unrighteousness."* **(1 John 1:9)**

- **Consecration:** Consecration means dedicating yourself, your life, and your efforts to God's will. This is a process of setting yourself apart for God. Holiness strengthens your spiritual authority. Spend prayer, fasting, and worship as a sign of your commitment. Without consecration, slipping back into old habits and opening the door for the enemy to return is easy.

Scripture Reference: *"Be holy, for I am holy."* (1 Peter 1:16)

- **Spiritual Covering:** It's essential to have spiritual covering. This could be a pastor, mentor, or someone in spiritual authority who can agree with you during this process. In Matthew 18:19, it says, *"If two of you agree on earth concerning anything that they ask, it will be done for them by My Father in heaven."* Having someone in agreement with you strengthens your position in battle.

Step 2: Identify the Demonic Altar

You cannot defeat what you cannot identify. Demonic altars are often tied to specific areas of struggle or patterns in your life. When you identify the source, you begin the process of dismantling it.

- **Ancestral Patterns**: Generational altars often influence entire bloodlines. These altars are rooted in ancestral practices, curses, or spiritual agreements passed down through the generations. Look for recurring struggles in your family, such as poverty, sickness, addiction, and failure. These generational issues may be directly connected to altars established by previous generations.

  Scripture Reference:

  "The iniquity of the father is visited upon the children to the third and fourth generations of those who hate Me." —**Exodus 20:5**

- **Emotional Ties**: Some altars are tied to deep emotional wounds, such as trauma from abuse, rejection, or abandonment. These wounds can provide the enemy with legal access points to bind you emotionally and spiritually. Examine your life for any emotional scars or toxic relationships that may have empowered an altar to operate in your life.

Scripture Reference:

"He heals the brokenhearted and binds up their wounds." —**Psalm 147:3**

- **Physical Locations**: Certain locations, such as ancestral homes, graveyards, or areas where occult practices took place, can serve as physical points of contact for demonic altars. These areas may still hold spiritual residue from past ungodly activities. Take time to evaluate if specific locations in your life or family history may have spiritual significance linked to idolatry, witchcraft, or other forms of dedication to evil spirits.

Scripture Reference: *"The earth is the Lord's, and the fullness thereof."*

—**Psalm 24:1**

Step 3: Renounce and Break the Covenant

Demonic altars operate on legal covenants, agreements, and sacrifices. These covenants are what empower the altar to continue influencing your life. Breaking these covenants is crucial.

- **Renounce the Altar's Influence**: When you renounce an altar, you declare that you no longer agree with its evil influence over your life. You are severing your connection to it in the spiritual realm. In the name of Jesus, declare: *"I renounce every covenant, dedication, or vow tied to this altar."*

- **Sever Legal Rights**: Through the blood of Jesus, you can sever every legal right that the altar holds over your life. As a believer, Christ has given you the authority to cancel any legal claim the enemy has over your life. Declare:

    "I sever every legal right this altar has over my life by the blood of Jesus."

Scripture Reference:

"Having canceled the written code, with its regulations, that was against us and that stood opposed to us; He took it away, nailing it to the cross." –-Colossians 2:14

Step 4: Destroy the Altar in Prayer

Now that you have renounced the altar and broken the covenant, you must destroy it through powerful prayer. Prayer is the most effective weapon you have in spiritual warfare.

- **Decree the Word of God**: Use scriptures as weapons to tear down the altar's influence. The Word is alive and powerful, and it has the authority to break every chain. Declare powerful scriptures over the altar, such as

  Isaiah 54:17,

  "No weapon formed against you shall prosper,"

  2 Corinthians 10:4-5,

  "For the weapons of our warfare are not carnal, but mighty in God for pulling down strongholds."

- **Command Fire from Heaven**: Pray for the consuming fire of God to destroy the altar. Just as Elijah called down fire to consume the altar of Baal **(1 Kings 18:38)**, you, too, can invoke the fire of God to burn up the evil structure.

Scripture Reference: *"Our God is a consuming fire."* —**Hebrews 12:29**

- **Declare the Name of Jesus**: Jesus is the ultimate authority. When you declare the name of Jesus, every knee bows, and every demon must flee. Proclaim His authority over the altar and the demonic spirits behind it.

Scripture Reference:

"At the name of Jesus, every knee should bow, in heaven and on earth and under the earth." —**Philippians 2:10**

Step 5: Uproot the Evil Foundation

Demonic altars are often built on deep, spiritual foundations rooted in sin, curses, or generational patterns. To prevent these altars from returning, you must address their root causes.

Generational Roots: Ask the Holy Spirit to reveal any hidden generational roots of the altar. These are the spiritual foundations that need to be uprooted. Break any bloodline curses and renounce ancestral ties that continue to give the altar power.

Establish New Foundations in Christ: Declare that your foundation is now in Christ and that every generational curse is broken. Your spiritual lineage is now established in the victory of Jesus Christ.

Scripture Reference: *"If anyone is in Christ, he is a new creation; old things have passed away; behold, all things have become new."* (2 Corinthians 5:17)

Step 6: Raise a Godly Altar in Its Place

Once the demonic altar is destroyed, replacing it with a godly altar is essential. This ensures there is no void for the enemy to return to.

Prayer Altar: Dedicate a place in your home or life to prayer. Set aside a specific time each day to meet with God. This will become your spiritual foundation, where you can commune with Him.

Worship Altar: Fill your life with worship. Worship invites God's presence; where His presence dwells, the enemy cannot remain.

Sacrificial Altar: Commit to a lifestyle of sacrificial worship. This includes fasting, sowing seeds of faith, and dedicating your time and resources to God's work.

Scripture Reference: *"I beseech you therefore, brethren, by the mercies of God, that you present your bodies a living sacrifice, holy, acceptable to God, which is your reasonable service."* (Romans 12:1)

Step 7: Maintain Your Victory

Deliverance is a continuous process that requires vigilance and spiritual discipline. To maintain your victory:

Daily Prayer and Declarations: Continue to speak God's Word over your life and declare His promises. This will help keep the enemy at bay and strengthen your faith.

Fellowship with Believers: Stay connected with a Bible-believing church and community. Surround yourself with believers who can support you and keep you accountable.

Guard Your Gates: Be mindful of what you allow into your life through relationships, media, and external influences. Guard your mind and spirit from anything that can allow the enemy to return.

Conclusion

Destroying demonic altars requires boldness, strategy, and perseverance. As you follow this step-by-step process, trust that God will grant you victory. Remember, no altar is greater than the name of Jesus. By His blood, you have already overcome! Stay firm in your authority, knowing God has equipped you with everything you need to walk in lasting freedom.

Closing Prayer:

Heavenly Father,

I thank You for the victory that is mine through Jesus Christ. I stand firm in Your authority and the power of Your Word. I declare that every demonic altar that has been erected against my life is destroyed by the fire of the Holy Spirit. Thank You for revealing the strategies of the enemy and empowering me to break free from every chain and stronghold.

As I continue in this journey of spiritual freedom, I commit to maintaining my deliverance through Your Word, prayer, and obedience. I ask for the wisdom and discernment to recognize any attempts by the enemy to regain ground in my life. Lord, fill me with Your Holy Spirit and guide me with divine strength and understanding.

I declare that I will walk in the fullness of Your victory, free from the influence of every demonic altar. Let Your peace, power, and presence be my constant source of strength. I seal this victory in Jesus' name, knowing that no weapon formed against me shall prosper.

Thank You, Lord, for the freedom and authority You have given me. I walk boldly in the purpose and destiny You have called me to. I believe that my best days are ahead, and that the altars of darkness have no power over my life.

In Jesus' mighty name,

Amen.

CHAPTER 7:
Ancestral and Territorial Altars: Breaking Generational Strongholds

Demonic altars tied to ancestry and territorial regions are among the most stubborn and deeply rooted spiritual strongholds. These altars are often established through bloodlines, family practices, and geographical control, enabling generational curses to persist across multiple lifetimes. Overcoming these requires strategic spiritual engagement and unwavering faith in God's power. In this chapter, we will break down how to identify and destroy these altars, reclaiming both your bloodline and the territories claimed by the enemy.

Understanding Ancestral Altars

Ancestral altars are spiritual platforms erected by previous generations, and they hold the power to influence current generations, often for decades or even centuries. These altars are built through practices, agreements, and dedication of families or individuals to spiritual forces outside God's will. The following are key elements that often make ancestral altars so deeply rooted:

- **Bloodline Curses:** These are recurring patterns of poverty, sickness, addiction, and broken relationships that repeat through family lines. The enemy uses these altars to enforce these curses, keeping generations trapped in cycles of defeat.

Scripture Reference:

"The iniquity of the fathers upon the children to the third and fourth generations of those who hate Me." **-Exodus 20:5**

- **Covenants and Dedications:** Past generations may have unknowingly dedicated their descendants to demonic entities through covenants, vows, or rituals, which give spiritual entities legal authority to operate in your bloodline.

Scripture Reference:

"But the things which God has prepared for those who love Him..." **—1 Corinthians 2:9**

This highlights the importance of covenant-breaking to bring forth God's blessings for your lineage.

- **Inherited Bondage:** Ancestral altars influence descendants, often keeping entire bloodlines in cycles of oppression, spiritual blindness, or limitation. The bondage passed down isn't always obvious but manifests in ways that hold back spiritual growth, prosperity, and peace.

Signs of Ancestral Altars in Operation

It is essential to identify when ancestral altars are operating in your life. These altars often manifest in ways that seem insurmountable and repetitive. Some signs include:

- **Persistent Patterns of Failure:** Despite prayer, effort, or hard work, there are recurring patterns of failure in your life. You may experience consistent financial setbacks, health issues, or relational struggles that seem to run in the family.

- **Frequent Encounters with Demonic Oppression**: If you find yourself experiencing nightmares, demonic visitations, or a sense of oppression that doesn't seem to have a natural explanation, it may be a sign that an ancestral altar is at work.

- **Spiritual Stagnation:** A resistance to spiritual growth or an unusual pattern of backsliding in your family or personal life. These strongholds can resist progress and spiritual maturity, making it harder to experience true freedom in Christ.

Breaking Ancestral Altars

Breaking ancestral altars requires intentional spiritual work and strategic action. Taking each step with faith and commitment to the process is essential. Here are the steps to begin the journey of breaking generational strongholds:

- **Identify the Root**: Ask the Holy Spirit to reveal the origin of the generational stronghold. It may be tied to specific sins, covenants, or rituals performed by ancestors. Reflect on family history, recurring issues, and areas of persistent struggle.

Scripture Reference:

"The Holy Spirit will guide you into all truth." —John 16:13

- **Renounce Ancestral Ties:** Declare out loud,

"I renounce every ungodly covenant, vow, or dedication tied to my bloodline."

Renouncing these ties disconnects you from the influence of the ancestral altar and breaks its power over you.

Scripture Reference:

"If the Son sets you free, you will be free indeed."
—John 8:36

- **Repent for Generational Sins:** Stand in the gap for your family and repent for the sins of past generations. Acknowledge the wrongs done by your ancestors, whether knowingly or unknowingly, and ask God to forgive them.

Scripture Reference:

"We have sinned, even as our fathers; we have done wrong and acted wickedly."

—Psalm 106:6

- **Destroy the Altar:** Command the altar to be broken by the fire of God, declaring:

"I command every demonic altar tied to my family line to be destroyed now in Jesus' name!"

Do not shy away from speaking with boldness, for the authority of Jesus is the power that destroys these altars.

Scripture Reference:

"I will build My church, and the gates of hell shall not prevail against it."

—Matthew 16:18

- **Declare Your New Identity**: After renouncing and breaking the power of ancestral altars, declare your new identity in Christ. Your bloodline is now purified through the blood of Jesus, and the curses of your ancestors no longer bind you.

Scripture Reference:

"You are a chosen generation, a royal priesthood, a holy nation, His own special people." —1 Peter 2:9

Understanding Territorial Altars

Territorial altars are spiritual strongholds over regions, cities, or territories. They seek to control the atmosphere and promote spiritual darkness, resistance to God's kingdom, and corruption. They can hinder spiritual growth and keep revival at bay.

- **Territorial Altars Promote Darkness**: These altars often resist the advancement of the Gospel, promote crime, immorality, and foster a climate of poverty or spiritual dryness in specific areas.

Biblical Example: In *Daniel 10*, the **"Prince of Persia"** was a territorial principality that resisted God's messenger, delaying Daniel's prayer. Territorial spirits can hinder God's work in specific regions.

Scripture Reference:

"The earth is the Lord's, and the fullness thereof."
—**Psalm 24:1**

Signs of Territorial Altars in Operation

You can often identify territorial altars through the struggles and oppression in specific regions or areas of influence. Some signs include:

- **Violence and Immorality**: Territorial altars often influence cities or regions plagued by continuous violence, moral decay, and widespread corruption.

- **Spiritual Heaviness:** A spiritual heaviness or resistance to ministry and growth, especially within churches or ministries, can signify that a territorial altar is in place.

- **Resistance to the Gospel**: Certain regions may consistently resist the Gospel, with the message struggling to take root in the people's hearts.

Breaking Territorial Altars

Breaking territorial altars requires bold prophetic intercession and acts of faith. Here are some steps to take:

- Engage in Prophetic Intercession: Pray over your city, region, or home, declaring God's sovereignty over the territory. Speak His authority into the atmosphere, declaring that every demonic influence must bow to the name of Jesus.

  Scripture Reference:

  "For the earth will be filled with the knowledge of the glory of the Lord, as the waters cover the sea."
  -Habakkuk 2:14

- **Declare God's Ownership:** Proclaim God's dominion over your territory, stating that

"The earth is the Lord's, and the fullness thereof."
—**Psalm 24:1**

Declare His reign and rule over the region, cities, or places affected by territorial altars.

- **Anoint the Land:** Anointing oil symbolizes the consecration of the land to God. Walk through your city or home, anointing the ground and declaring that the area belongs to God's kingdom.

Scripture Reference:

"The anointing breaks the yoke." —Isaiah 10:27

- **Raise a Godly Altar:** Establish an altar of prayer, worship, and thanksgiving to invite God's presence. This act creates an atmosphere of spiritual authority and peace, reducing the influence of territorial altars.

Prayer for Breaking Ancestral and Territorial Altars

Father, in the name of Jesus, I take authority over every ancestral and territorial altar established against my life, family, and region. I renounce every demonic covenant, dedication, and agreement tied to my bloodline. I break their power now by the blood of Jesus. I declare that the fire of God consumes every evil altar. I claim my freedom and establish a new altar of worship, prayer, and dedication to You. Let Your kingdom reign in my life, family, and city. In Jesus' name, Amen.

Conclusion

Breaking ancestral and territorial altars requires boldness, persistence, and strategic prayer. You will walk in freedom and victory by identifying the strongholds, renouncing ungodly ties, confronting these altars with the Word of God, and establishing new godly altars. Remember, Jesus has already won the ultimate victory, and you are empowered to overcome through His name. No altar—be it ancestral or territorial—can stand against the name of Jesus. Continue standing firm in His power, knowing you are victorious.

Part 3

Rising in Power and Dominion

CHAPTER 8:
Total Freedom: Deliverance and Maintaining Your Spiritual Victory

Achieving deliverance is just the beginning of your journey. Maintaining your spiritual victory is key to walking in sustained freedom. Deliverance is not a one-time event but a continuous process that requires vigilance, spiritual discipline, and a transformed lifestyle. This chapter will explore securing lasting freedom and ensuring the enemy does not regain access to your life.

Step 1: Understand the Nature of Deliverance

Deliverance is not merely about casting out demonic forces—it is about total healing, restoration, and the renewal of your mind. Jesus declared in ***John 8:36,***

"If the Son makes you free, you will be free indeed."

This freedom is comprehensive; it includes the freedom of your mind, emotions, relationships, and destiny.

Deliverance provides a spiritual reset—a new beginning. The moment you are set free, you are no longer bound by the chains that once held you. However, this freedom must be understood and maintained. Deliverance is not just about removing evil forces but about **receiving the fullness** of what God has for you—peace, joy, and purpose.

Step 2: Close Every Open Door

After deliverance, the enemy will attempt to regain access to your life. This is why maintaining vigilance and addressing open doors is essential to ensuring your freedom is not short-lived.

- **Repent and Renounce**: Sin, occult practices, and ungodly relationships can open doors for the enemy. Repentance is the first line of defense. Renounce any past ties, agreements, or practices that give the enemy legal access to your life. This includes renouncing occult practices, soul ties, and any other unbiblical agreements. Speak out loud and break all agreements with the enemy.

Scripture Reference:

"If we confess our sins, He is faithful and just to forgive us our sins and to cleanse us from all unrighteousness."
-1 John 1:9

- **Cancel Legal Rights**: Demons often gain access through legal rights such as unforgiveness, bitterness, or unconfessed sin. If these issues are not addressed, they provide a foothold for the enemy to return. Cancel these rights by applying the blood of Jesus through prayer and confession.

Scripture Reference:

"And they overcame him by the blood of the Lamb and by the word of their testimony..." —**Revelation 12:11**

- **Guard Your Environment**: The atmosphere around you plays a significant role in maintaining your freedom. Remove any objects, media, or influences that invite darkness into your home. This could include music, books, movies, or entertainment glorifying sin or demonic activity. Protect your home as a sanctuary for God's presence.

Scripture Reference:

"Do not give the devil a foothold." —Ephesians 4:27

Step 3: Establish Daily Spiritual Discipline

Victory is maintained through consistent spiritual discipline. Without a daily commitment to prayer, Bible study, and worship, slipping back into old patterns is easy. Here's how to keep your spiritual life strong:

- **Prayer and Intercession:** Develop a consistent prayer routine. Your prayer life serves as a shield, protecting you from spiritual attacks. The more you commune with God, the more you invite His protection and guidance.

  Scripture Reference:

  "Pray without ceasing." —1 Thessalonians 5:17)

- **Studying the Word:** God's Word is sharper than any two-edged sword, and it is your primary weapon for spiritual defense. Immerse yourself daily in Scripture. Let the Word of God renew your mind and guide your decisions.

Scripture Reference:

"For the word of God is living and active, sharper than any two-edged sword..." —Hebrews 4:12

- **Worship and Praise**: Worship is a powerful weapon against the enemy. It invites God's presence into your life and creates an atmosphere where demonic forces cannot thrive. Praise shifts your focus from your problems to God's greatness.

Scripture Reference:

"God inhabits the praises of His people." —Psalm 22:3

Step 4: Develop Godly Relationships

Spiritual growth is enhanced through connection with other believers. As you walk out your deliverance, you must surround yourself with a support system of godly individuals who can hold you accountable, pray with you, and encourage you in times of spiritual warfare.

- **Accountability**: Seek relationships where you can be transparent and honest about your struggles. Accountability helps keep you on track and provides spiritual strength when you face challenges.

Scripture Reference:

"Iron sharpens iron, so one person sharpens another." —Proverbs 27:17

- **Praying Together**: Develop a prayer partnership with others committed to spiritual growth. When you pray together, your prayers are more powerful, and you can agree on your spiritual battles.

Scripture Reference:

"For where two or three gather in my name, there am I with them." —Matthew 18:20

- **Encouragement in Warfare**: Walking in victory requires encouragement. Find others who will lift you when you feel weak and remind you of the truth of God's Word during difficult times.

Step 5: Guard Your Mind and Emotions

The enemy often attacks through mental and emotional strongholds, aiming to steal your peace and hinder your spiritual progress. Protecting your mind and emotions is key to maintaining your deliverance.

- **Renew Your Thoughts**: Meditate on God's promises and renew your mind with His truth. What you focus on grows stronger, so keep your thoughts aligned with God's Word.

Scripture Reference:

"Do not conform to the pattern of this world, but be transformed by the renewing of your mind." —**Romans 12:2**

- **Declare Affirmations**: Speak life-giving affirmations that align with God's Word. Every time negative thoughts arise, counter them with the truth of God's promises.

Scripture Reference:

"You will also declare a thing, and it will be established for you." —**Job 22:28**

- **Cast Down Imaginations**: Reject the enemy's lies and take authority over your thoughts. If the enemy whispers lies, replace those lies with the truth of God's Word. Command every thought to align with Christ.

Scripture Reference:

"We demolish arguments and every pretension that sets itself up against the knowledge of God, and we take captive every thought to make it obedient to Christ."

—2 Corinthians 10:5

Step 6: Raise a Godly Altar

To maintain freedom, you must establish a godly altar in your home. This altar represents your dedication to God and serves as a spiritual stronghold in your life.

- **Prayer Altar**: Designate a specific space for prayer and intercession. This is where you meet with God daily, allowing Him to speak into your life and strengthen your spirit.

- **Worship Altar**: Establish an atmosphere of worship in your home. Fill your space with songs that glorify God, creating an environment where His presence dwells and the enemy cannot remain.

- **Sacrificial Altar**: Commit to a lifestyle of sacrificial worship, whether through fasting, giving, or serving. This dedication strengthens your spiritual authority and keeps the enemy at bay.

Scripture Reference:

"I urge you, brothers and sisters, in view of God's mercy, to offer your bodies as a living sacrifice, holy and pleasing to God." **—Romans 12:1**

Step 7: Walk in Your New Identity

Embrace and declare your new identity in Christ. You are no longer a slave to sin and oppression; you are a child of God, seated in heavenly places with Christ. This new identity is the foundation of your spiritual victory.

- **Declare Your Freedom**: Speak daily affirmations that reinforce your new identity in Christ. Declare the truth of God's Word over your life and your circumstances.

   Scripture Reference:

   "Now if we are children, then we are heirs—heirs of God and co-heirs with Christ." **—Romans 8:17**

- **Walk in Your Authority**: Understand that as a believer, you have been given authority over all the enemy's power. Stand firm in this authority, knowing the enemy has no right to touch your life.

Scripture Reference:

"I have given you authority...to overcome all the power of the enemy." —Luke 10:19

Step 8: Maintain a Spirit of Thanksgiving

Gratitude is a powerful tool for maintaining your freedom. Thanksgiving shifts your focus from your struggles to God's victories. It creates an atmosphere of faith and draws you closer to God's presence.

- **Constant Praise**: Maintain a heart of gratitude and praise, continually thanking God for the victory He has given you. Praise not only strengthens you but also pushes back the darkness.

Scripture Reference:

"Enter His gates with thanksgiving, and His courts with praise." —Psalm 100:4

Prayer for Total Freedom

Father, in the name of Jesus, I thank You for the deliverance You have brought into my life. I declare that every chain is broken, and every altar raised against me is destroyed. I close every door to the enemy and claim my place in Your kingdom. Surround me with Your presence, fill my home with peace, and guard my heart with Your Word. I walk in victory, freedom, and dominion. In Jesus' name, Amen.

Conclusion

Total freedom is sustained through vigilance, prayer, and a commitment to spiritual growth. By closing demonic access points, establishing godly altars, and walking in your God-given identity, you will maintain your victory and live in the fullness of God's promises. Remember, true freedom is not just being delivered from oppression but living empowered by the Holy Spirit in total victory.

CHAPTER 9:
Rebuilding Godly Altars: Establishing Divine Foundations

In the previous chapters, we discussed demonic altars' destructive power, operation, and the steps required to break free from their grip. As we move toward complete spiritual freedom and restoration, we must focus on rebuilding what was once lost, the Godly altars that connect us to the divine. A Godly altar serves as a place of encounter, transformation, and worship, where we invite God to dwell and reign in our lives. It is the foundation of our relationship with the Almighty, and it has the power to establish the kingdom of heaven on earth in our personal lives, families, and communities.

The Importance of Godly Altars

A Godly altar is a sacred place where we consecrate ourselves before God. It is the foundation upon which we build our faith and seek God's presence. In the Bible, altars were built as places of sacrifice and worship, where God's people would offer themselves in surrender and devotion. These altars were physical structures and symbolic of the heart's dedication to God's will.

- **Biblical Example**: In *Genesis 8:20*, Noah built an altar after the flood to offer a sacrifice of thanksgiving to God. This worship marked a new beginning for humanity, and the altar was a sign of gratitude and dedication.

- **Abraham's Altar**: In *Genesis 12:7-8*, Abraham built altars wherever he went as a sign of his covenant with God and his trust in divine promises. These altars were not mere rituals but places where Abraham encountered God and received divine revelation.

Altars are not just a religious practice but are foundational to spiritual victory. They determine what we invite into our lives. If we build an altar unto God, we open the door for His presence, power, and favor to flow into our lives. But if we leave our altars neglected or allow them to be defiled, we also invite spiritual chaos and instability.

Rebuilding the Altar of Your Heart

The first altar we must rebuild is the altar of our hearts. Over time, we may have allowed sin, offense, neglect, or disobedience to erode the sacred space within us that was once dedicated to God. The altar of the heart is where the true transformation begins, and it must be restored for us to experience the fullness of God's presence and power.

1. **Repentance and Cleansing**: The first step in rebuilding the altar of your heart is repentance. Repentance is not just an acknowledgment of sin but an intentional turning away from it. It is a profound sorrow for the things that have grieved God's heart and a decision to consecrate our lives entirely to Him. We must ask the Holy Spirit to show us where we have defiled our hearts with idolatry, unforgiveness, pride, or other sins. Once we recognize these areas, we must bring them before God in repentance and allow Him to cleanse us.

   Scripture Reference:

   "Create in me a clean heart, O God, and renew a steadfast spirit within me." —**Psalm 51:10**)

2. **Prayer and Consecration**: After repentance, the next step is consecration—dedicating ourselves to God's purposes. Consecration involves surrendering our lives, ambitions, and desires to God. In this sacred space of consecration, prayer becomes vital. Prayer invites God's presence into our lives and aligns our hearts with His will.

Scripture Reference:

"Consecrate yourselves, for tomorrow the Lord will do amazing things among you." —Joshua 3:5

3. **Building a Lifestyle of Worship**: Worship is the language of the altar. To rebuild a Godly altar, we must cultivate a lifestyle of worship that glorifies God in everything we do. Worship is not confined to songs on Sundays but is a daily act of surrender. It is reflected in our decisions, relationships, work, and lives. When we live with a heart of worship, we continually invite God's presence into our lives.

Scripture Reference:

"Therefore I urge you, brothers and sisters, in view of God's mercy, to offer your bodies as a living sacrifice,

holy and pleasing to God—this is your true and proper worship." —Romans 12:1

4. **Surrendering Our Sacrifice**: In the Old Testament, altars were places of sacrifice. While we no longer offer animal sacrifices, we are still called to offer ourselves as living sacrifices to God. Rebuilding the altar of our hearts requires laying down our personal ambitions, desires, and pride before God. This act of surrender enables God to mold us for His purposes.

Scripture Reference:

"I beseech you therefore, brethren, by the mercies of God, that you present your bodies as a living sacrifice, holy, acceptable to God, which is your reasonable service." —Romans 12:1

Rebuilding Altars in Your Family and Household

As we rebuild the altar of our hearts, we must also restore the altars in our homes. Our families are meant to be places where God's presence dwells and His power manifests in every area. Just as altars were built in biblical figures like Noah, Abraham, and Isaac's homes, so should we build altars in our homes.

1. **Family Consecration**: Rebuilding an altar in your home begins with consecrating your family to God. Gather your family together and dedicate each member to the Lord. This can be done through prayer, worship, and seeking God's guidance as a family unit. Speak words of blessing over your family and declare unity, healing, and breakthrough in your household.

   Scripture Reference:

   "As for me and my house, we will serve the Lord." —**Joshua 24:15**

2. **Family Worship and Prayer**: Establishing a family prayer and worship routine is crucial for rebuilding godly altars in the home. This could be as simple as having regular prayer times, reading Scripture together, and singing worship songs. Invite God's presence to fill your home, bringing peace, joy, and protection to every member of the family.

   Scripture Reference:

   "Where two or three are gathered in my name, there am I with them." —**Matthew 18:20**

3. **Breaking Ungodly Altars in the Home**: In many families, there may be generational altars that have been passed down through the bloodline, altars of dysfunction, addiction, or idolatry. To rebuild a godly altar, we must first identify and break any ungodly altars operating in the family line. This requires prayer, repentance, and the application of spiritual warfare to sever ties with these altars.

Scripture Reference:

"The God of Abraham, the God of Isaac, and the God of Jacob." —**Exodus 3:6**

Rebuilding Altars in the Community and Church

As we restore Godly altars in our hearts and homes, we must extend this restoration to our communities and churches. Altars are not only personal but corporate. The body of Christ is called to be an altar where God's presence dwells and His will is done on earth as it is in heaven.

1. **Church Revival**: Just as we have built altars in our personal lives, we must also call for a revival in the church. This revival begins with prayer, repentance, and a reestablishment of a passion for God's presence. When

the church becomes a place of true worship, it becomes a beacon of light in the community and an altar for all who seek God's healing and deliverance.

Scripture Reference:

"And the Lord added to their number daily those who were being saved." —Acts 2:47

2. **Community Impact:** The altars we rebuild in our lives and churches should not be confined to four walls. We are called to impact our communities, bringing the power of the altar to those in need. As we consecrate our lives to God, we become instruments of change in our neighborhoods, workplaces, and nations. Our lives should reflect the power of God's presence, drawing others to Him.

Scripture Reference:

"You are the light of the world." —Matthew 5:14

Conclusion

Rebuilding godly altars is essential to establishing divine foundations in our lives. It is a process that requires intentionality, sacrifice, and dedication. As we restore the altar of our hearts, homes, and communities, we create spaces where God's presence can dwell, transformation can take place, and His kingdom can advance. Remember, an altar is not just a place but a lifestyle. Rebuild the altar, and watch God establish His divine foundations in every area of your life.

Closing Prayer:

Father, in the mighty name of Jesus, I come before You with a heart full of gratitude for the wisdom and revelation You have provided in this chapter. Thank you for reminding me of the importance of rebuilding godly altars in my heart, home, and community. I recognize that you are the foundation of everything; I can do nothing without you.

Lord, as I have learned, I ask You to help me restore the altar of my heart. Remove any impurities, distractions, or sins that have defiled this sacred place. I repent every time I allow other things to take precedence over You. Cleanse my heart and make it pure, consecrated, and fully dedicated to Your will.

I consecrate my life to You, O God. I invite Your Holy Spirit to fill my heart, home, and environment. May I live in constant worship, continually offering myself as a living sacrifice, holy and pleasing to You. I lay down my desires, ambitions, and pride and surrender fully to Your divine purposes.

Father, I ask that You strengthen me to rebuild the altars in my home, family, and church. May your presence fill every room, bringing unity, peace, healing, and restoration to every relationship and every family. I declare that no demonic altar will have a hold over my home, and that Your power and presence will reign supreme.

Lord, help me to be a vessel of transformation in my community and the world. As I rebuild these altars, let them be places where Your kingdom advances, Your light shines, and Your love and power touch lives.

I commit to maintaining these altars with dedication, discipline, and vigilance. I promise to guard the sacred space where I encounter You, always inviting You into every area of my life.

Thank you, Father, for hearing my prayer and for the victory that is mine in Christ Jesus. You will establish your divine foundations in every area of my life, family, and community. Let your will be done on earth as it is in heaven.

In Jesus' mighty name, I pray. Amen.

CHAPTER 10:
Living in Unshakable Spiritual Victory

In the previous chapters, we've explored the **depth of spiritual warfare,** the destruction caused by demonic altars, and the essential steps required to break free from their strongholds. We've also covered the rebuilding of godly altars, which are the foundation of our spiritual restoration and growth. Now, we come to the culmination of this journey—living in unshakable spiritual victory.

To live in unshakable spiritual victory means to stand firm, unyielding, and victorious, no matter the storms or battles that may come your way. It means possessing a faith and resilience rooted in the power of God, where His promises are more accurate than any opposition, and where you can declare with confidence that you are more than a conqueror in Christ **(*Romans 8:37*).**

The Nature of Unshakable Spiritual Victory

Unshakable spiritual victory is not the absence of trials or difficulties. Victory becomes most evident when we face challenges and overcome them. A victorious mindset and lifestyle allow us to navigate life's challenges with unrelenting faith, knowing God is with us every step. This victory is born from the following:

1. Standing on the Authority of Christ

The foundation of unshakable spiritual victory is rooted in Christ's authority over every believer. Jesus declared,

"All authority in heaven and on earth has been given to me" —*Matthew 28:18*

As His followers, we have access to that same authority. The enemy may try to attack, deceive, or disrupt our peace, but we are armed with the authority of Christ. This means that **every weapon the enemy forms against us will not prosper (*Isaiah 54:17*). We are seated in heavenly places with Christ (*Ephesians 2:6*),** and from this vantage point, we stand firm, knowing that no enemy can defeat us.

2. Understanding Your Position in Christ

To live in unshakable victory, it is critical to understand who you are in Christ. Your identity in Him gives you the strength to persevere. As a child of God, you are clothed with Christ's righteousness and called to live in the fullness of His promises. Understanding your divine identity gives you the confidence to face any spiritual battle, knowing that your victory is already secured in Christ.

When you walk in the fullness of your identity in Christ, you understand that the victory has already been won. You do not fight from a place of defeat, but from a position of victory. **Jesus has already triumphed over death, sin, and the powers of darkness on the cross (*Colossians 2:15*).** Your role is to enforce His victory on earth.

3. Empowered by the Holy Spirit

Unshakable victory is not something we achieve in our strength. The Holy Spirit is the power source that enables us to overcome every obstacle. When the enemy comes to attack, the Spirit of God empowers us to stand firm. The Bible tells us that **the Holy Spirit is our Helper, Comforter, and the one who equips us for battle (*John 14:26, Ephesians 6:10-11*).** We can discern the enemy's strategies with His guidance and walk in divine wisdom to overcome them.

The Holy Spirit also gives us the **fruit of the Spirit—love, joy, peace, patience, kindness, goodness, faithfulness, gentleness, and self-control (*Galatians 5:22-23*)**, all weapons of victory. When we walk in the Spirit, we walk in victory. We are no longer slaves to fear, but we live with boldness, confidence, and courage, knowing that the Spirit empowers us to succeed.

4. Trusting in God's Faithfulness

Unshakable victory also comes from trusting in the unchanging faithfulness of God. Throughout Scripture, we see repeatedly how God is faithful to His promises. In *2 Corinthians 1:20*, we are reminded that **"all the promises of God are yes and amen in Christ Jesus."** When we face trials, we can stand firm knowing that God is faithful to bring us to victory. The Apostle Paul said it best: **"If God is for us, who can be against us?" (*Romans 8:31*).** God's promises will never fail, and His Word is a firm foundation upon which we can build our victory.

The Key Elements to Living in Unshakable Victory

To live in unshakable spiritual victory, there are specific keys to apply in your life that will anchor you in the victory God has promised:

1. A Lifestyle of Prayer and Fasting

Prayer is our direct line of communication with God. Through prayer, we receive direction, strength, and strategy for life's battles. Jesus modeled the power of persistent prayer (***Luke 18:1***), and we are called to follow His example. Fasting is a powerful tool that aligns our hearts with God's will and brings breakthroughs in spiritual warfare. Together, prayer and fasting help us remain grounded in our victory.

2. Speaking the Word of God

The Word of God is alive and powerful and our primary weapon in the spiritual battle. When the enemy comes against us, we must respond with the truth of God's Word. Jesus, when tempted by Satan in the wilderness, responded with Scripture, declaring the Word over every temptation (***Matthew 4:1-11***). Speaking the Word of God aligns our hearts with His will and solidifies our victory.

3. Worship and Praise

Worship is one of the most powerful forms of spiritual warfare. When we praise God, we invite His presence into our circumstances. The Bible tells us that **God inhabits the praises of His people (*Psalm 22:3*).** When we worship, we shift our focus from the problem to the problem-solver.

Worship aligns us with God's victory, and it helps us remember His faithfulness.

4. Maintaining a Spirit of Gratitude

Gratitude is a powerful tool in maintaining spiritual victory. Regardless of our battles, gratitude shifts our perspective and positions us to receive more from God. By giving thanks in all circumstances, we acknowledge God's sovereignty over our lives and declare He is greater than any opposition. Gratitude strengthens our faith and keeps us focused on the goodness of God.

5. Walking in Love and Forgiveness

Walking in love and forgiveness is one of the most vital elements in maintaining spiritual victory. The enemy thrives in environments of bitterness, unforgiveness, and offense. However, when we walk in love, we disarm the enemy's ability to divide and conquer. Jesus taught us to **forgive as He has forgiven us (*Matthew 6:14-15*). Love and forgiveness are weapons** that keep us unshakable in the face of trials.

Overcoming Obstacles and Trials

Living in unshakable spiritual victory does not mean we won't face trials or obstacles. The opposite is true: the more we advance in the kingdom of God, the more we will encounter resistance from the enemy. However, we are called to rejoice in the midst of trials because they **strengthen our faith and produce perseverance (*James 1:2-4*)**. When we encounter obstacles, we must remember that **God is working everything for our good (*Romans 8:28*)** and that every trial allows our faith to grow stronger.

The Ultimate Victory

The ultimate victory we have in Christ is eternal. Jesus has already won the battle over sin, death, and the enemy on the cross. The victory we experience in this life reflects that ultimate, eternal victory. When we live with the awareness that **we are already seated in heavenly places with Christ (*Ephesians 2:6*),** we can face any challenge confidently, knowing that our victory is secure in Him.

Conclusion

Living in unshakable spiritual victory is not a passive process. It requires intentionality, faith, and an active relationship with God. By standing firm in Christ's authority, understanding our position in Him, and relying on the power of the Holy Spirit, we can walk in the victory that Christ has already secured for us. With a lifestyle of prayer, praise, and gratitude, we can overcome obstacles and live unshakably victorious in every area of life. As we continue to enforce God's victory in our lives, we advance His kingdom on earth, and we stand as a testimony of His power, glory, and faithfulness.

As we close this book, I trust that you now understand the power and significance of altars in your life, both the ones that have bound you and the ones that have the potential to set you free. This journey of discovery is not just an academic pursuit—it is a spiritual awakening, a call to action that will alter the course of your life and impact those around you.

Closing Prayer:

Father, in the name of Jesus, I come before You with a heart of gratitude, knowing that You have already secured my victory. Thank you for the unshakable spiritual victory I have through the finished work of Jesus Christ. I declare that I am more than a conqueror in Him, and that no weapon formed against me shall prosper.

Lord, I thank You for reminding me of my authority in Christ, the empowerment of the Holy Spirit, and the truth of Your promises. I stand firm in my identity in You, trusting that You are with me every step of the way. I will not be moved by the trials or obstacles that come my way, for I know You are more significant than anything the enemy can bring.

I ask You to strengthen me, Lord, to walk in this victory daily. Help me to maintain a lifestyle of prayer, worship, and gratitude. May Your Word continue to be a lamp to my feet and a light to my path. I choose to speak Your promises over my life and to walk boldly in the authority You've given me.

Holy Spirit, empower me to live in unshakable victory. Guide me in every decision, strengthen my faith, and fill me with Your peace. I surrender my will to You and ask for Your wisdom and guidance in all that I do.

I declare that the enemy has no place in my life, family, or destiny. I stand in the victory that Christ has already won for me. I will not be swayed or shaken; I am rooted in Your promises and power.

Thank you, Father, for my victory in Christ. I walk in freedom, peace, and joy, knowing I am seated in heavenly places with Him. As I continue this journey, I declare that I will live in unshakable spiritual victory, advancing Your kingdom and being a light to others.

In Jesus' name, I pray. Amen.

Final Words: Walking in Your Destiny

As you have walked through the pages of this book, you have been equipped with powerful spiritual tools to confront and dismantle every demonic altar in your life. You've learned the importance of understanding and applying the authority given to you in Christ, and you now stand in a position of victory. The enemy no longer has legal rights over your life or destiny. You have been set free; that freedom is yours to claim and walk in daily.

But remember—this journey does not end here. It is just the beginning. Deliverance is a process, and maintaining the victory you've received requires constant vigilance, a lifestyle of prayer, worship, and daily surrender to God's will. The spiritual victory you've attained must be guarded, nurtured, and fortified with godly altars that invite His presence into every area of your life.

Past strongholds or generational curses no longer bind you. Your identity in Christ has been restored, and with it comes the power to transform your life and those around you. As you continue to walk in the fullness of God's promises, let your life testify to His power to break chains and destroy altars.

You are called to stand firm in the face of adversity, knowing that you are not fighting for victory, but from victory. Every day, as you declare God's Word, engage in spiritual warfare, and live in the authority Christ has given you, you will see the manifestation of His promises unfold in your life.

You have been chosen to rise above every altar of destruction and walk in the fullness of God's purpose for you. Let this book guide you, but let your relationship with the Holy Spirit be your constant companion, teacher, and guide. You are more than a conqueror, and your victory is assured in Christ.

As you close this book, let the journey of transformation continue. The power to break free, to rebuild godly altars, and to live in unshakable spiritual victory is within you. You are equipped, empowered, and ready to face every challenge confidently, knowing that all things are possible with God.

May you walk boldly in your divine purpose, with the authority of Christ, and the unshakable victory He has already secured for you. It is time to step into the fullness of your destiny.

God bless you, and may His peace, power, and presence be with you always.

Definitions:

Ancestral: Pertaining to one's ancestors or forebears. In spiritual contexts, this term often relates to the generational patterns, behaviors, or influences passed down through family lines, whether positive or negative.

Ancestral Iniquities: Sins or negative patterns of behavior passed down through generations. These iniquities can affect individuals, families, or entire bloodlines, manifesting as recurring cycles of curses, afflictions, or spiritual bondage.

Ancestral Practices are customs, traditions, or rituals passed down through generations that often have cultural, religious, or spiritual significance. These practices can include beneficial or harmful behaviors and beliefs rooted in ancestral heritage.

Authority in Christ: The power, right, and ability given to believers through their relationship with Jesus Christ to exercise spiritual dominion over the forces of darkness. This authority is rooted in Christ's victory over sin, death, and demonic powers.

Covenants are binding agreements or promises, often involving sacrifices, that establish legal rights or commitments. In a spiritual context, covenants can refer to agreements made with God or with the enemy that govern the spiritual destiny of individuals, families, or nations.

Demonic Altars: Spiritual structures or platforms built by demonic forces to establish dominion, enforce curses, and perpetuate spiritual bondage in a person's life, family, or territory. These altars often arise from sin, occult practices, or generational iniquities.

Deliverance: The act of being freed from spiritual bondage, oppression, or demonic influence through the power of Jesus Christ. It involves breaking curses, tearing down strongholds, and establishing godly altars for spiritual victory.

Demonic Influence is the power or presence of evil spirits that seek to manipulate, control, or harm individuals, families, or communities. Demonic influence operates through various spiritual entry points, including sin, occult practices, and unbroken generational curses.

Divine Authority: The supreme spiritual power granted by God to believers, enabling them to enforce His will on earth. It is the God-given right to command, bind, and loose in the spiritual realm, operating by God's will.

Generational Curses are spiritual consequences or negative patterns passed down from generation to generation, often due to sin or disobedience. These curses can manifest in various forms, including sickness, poverty, addiction, and relational dysfunction.

Godly Altars: Sacred places or spiritual platforms where individuals or communities dedicate themselves to God in worship, sacrifice, and service. These altars invite God's presence and blessings and serve as points of divine encounter.

Legal Rights: Spiritual entitlements or claims the enemy may hold over a person's life due to sin, disobedience, or unrepentant actions. These rights grant demonic forces legal access to influence or oppress an individual or family.

Prayer and Intercession: The act of communicating with God through spoken or silent prayer, seeking His intervention, guidance, or action in the lives of individuals or situations. Intercession specifically refers to praying on behalf of others.

Repentance: A deep, heartfelt turning away from sin and toward God. It involves sorrow for wrong actions, a decision to change one's ways, and a commitment to align with God's will.

Spiritual Warfare: The ongoing battle between the forces of good (God and His angels) and evil (Satan and his demons). Spiritual warfare involves the believer's active engagement in prayer, declarations, and actions to dismantle demonic strongholds and enforce God's kingdom on earth.

Strongholds are spiritual fortresses or areas of the mind, emotions, or life held captive by demonic forces. They are built through unrepentant sin, lies, and wrong thinking and must be torn down through prayer and spiritual warfare.

Territorial Altars: Spiritual strongholds established over specific geographic regions or territories. These altars control the spiritual atmosphere of an area and often resist the advancement of God's kingdom, promoting darkness, immorality, and oppression.

The Blood of Jesus: The powerful, redemptive sacrifice of Jesus Christ on the cross, which has the power to cleanse, protect, and break the legal rights of the enemy. The blood of Jesus is the ultimate weapon against spiritual oppression and demonic forces.

Unshakable Victory: A spiritual triumph where believers remain steadfast and victorious, despite external challenges or opposition. This victory is rooted in the authority of Christ, the empowerment of the Holy Spirit, and the unshakable promises of God.

APPENDIX A
Quick Reference Guide to Prayers for Deliverance

1. Prayer for Divine Insight and Revelation

Heavenly Father,

I come before You with a heart full of gratitude and anticipation. Lord, I ask that You would open the eyes of my understanding, giving me divine insight and revelation into the truth of Your Word. Illuminate every area of my life where I need deliverance and freedom. Expose every demonic altar that has held me bound, and reveal Your plan for my total restoration.

Holy Spirit, guide me through this journey of spiritual freedom. Help me discern the enemy's strategies and empower me to break free from the chains that have held me captive. I trust in Your wisdom and grace as I walk through this process of healing and restoration.

In Jesus' mighty name, Amen.

2. Prayer for Breaking the Power of Demonic Altars

Lord Jesus,

Thank you for the victory you secured for me on the cross. Today, I stand in the authority you gave me as a believer. I declare that every demonic altar set up against my life, my family, and my destiny is destroyed in the name of Jesus.

I renounce every covenant and agreement made with the enemy through these altars. I sever every tie and every chain that has bound me to demonic influences. I command every altar to be consumed by the fire of the Holy Ghost, and I declare that my life is free from every spiritual stronghold.

Father, I plead the blood of Jesus over my mind, body, and soul. I decree that I can fulfill the purpose You have ordained for me. Let every demonic legal right be revoked, and may Your divine purpose be established in my life.

In the name of Jesus Christ, Amen.

3. Prayer for Deliverance from Generational Curses

Heavenly Father,

I humbly come before You, acknowledging that You are the God who delivers and redeems. I repent for every known and unknown sin committed by my ancestors that has opened the door to generational curses. I confess the sins of my bloodline and ask for Your forgiveness.

Today, by the authority of Jesus Christ, I break the power of every generational curse passed down through my family line. I declare that these curses are null and void. Every curse of poverty, sickness, failure, addiction, and bondage is broken in the name of Jesus.

I release the blessing of the Lord into my life and the lives of my descendants. I decree that I am free from every demonic stronghold in my bloodline. May your blessings now flow through my generations, bringing restoration, peace, and favor.

Thank You, Father, for setting me free. In Jesus' name, Amen.

4. Prayer for Deliverance from Spiritual Bondage

Lord Jesus,

I come before You today, acknowledging Your power to set me free. I recognize that you are the Breaker who destroys every chain and prison the enemy has built in my life. I ask you to break every spiritual bondage that has kept me in a place of captivity.

I renounce every lie of the enemy that has held me in bondage and declare that I am free in Christ. I refuse to be a slave to sin, fear, rejection, shame, or any other spiritual stronghold.

I command every evil spirit that has tormented my soul to leave now, in the name of Jesus. I claim victory over every demonic influence in my life, and I declare that I am fully delivered and restored.

Holy Spirit, fill me with Your power and presence, and let me walk in the freedom Christ has purchased for me.

In Jesus' name, Amen.

5. Prayer for Rebuilding Godly Altars

Father God,

I thank you for the opportunity to rebuild godly altars in my life. I surrender myself to You as a living sacrifice, holy and acceptable, which is my reasonable service **(Romans 12:1)**. I dedicate every area of my life to You—my mind, body, soul, and spirit.

Lord, I invite You to establish Your altar in my heart and home. I ask that You pour out Your anointing upon me, that I may be a vessel used for Your glory. May the altar of worship be restored in my life, and may it be a place where Your presence dwells continually.

Remove every idol and false altar that has taken Your place in my life. Let Your fire consume every area that is not aligned with Your will, and may I offer up sacrifices of praise, prayer, and obedience unto You.

I commit to living a life of worship, intercession, and devotion, making my heart a place where You can dwell and speak. Let your altar be the foundation of my spiritual journey, and may I walk in the freedom and power it brings.

In Jesus' name, Amen.

6. Prayer for Living in Unshakable Spiritual Victory

Almighty God,

I praise You for the victory You have won for me through Christ. Today, I stand firm in Your victory, knowing that You have given me power and authority over every work of the enemy. I refuse to be shaken by the trials or storms that may come, for my foundation is built on the Rock—Jesus Christ.

I declare that no weapon formed against me shall prosper, and I condemn every tongue that rises against me in judgment **(Isaiah 54:17).** I walk in the victory that Christ has secured for me, and I hold fast to the promises You have given me.

Holy Spirit, empower me to remain strong, steadfast, and unmovable in adversity. Fill me with courage, peace, and strength to overcome every challenge.

I declare I am victorious in every area of my life, and the enemy's schemes will not move me. I am more than a conqueror through Christ, who loves me.

In Jesus' name, Amen.

7. Prayer for Continuous Freedom and Deliverance

Lord,

I thank you for the freedom and deliverance I have received through the blood of Jesus. I acknowledge that my victory is secure in You, and I commit to walking in that freedom daily.

I ask for your continued grace and strength as I walk this path of freedom. Protect me from the enemy's schemes and keep me close to You. Let Your Holy Spirit guide me in all things, and may I never return to the chains of bondage.

Help me remain vigilant, watching for any signs of spiritual attack. Give me the wisdom to recognize and resist the enemy's lies. I submit every area of my life to You, Lord, and I trust You to continue the work of deliverance in me.

Thank you for the freedom I have in Christ. May I walk in the fullness of that freedom every day.

In Jesus' name, Amen.

8. Prayer for Breaking Soul Ties and Unhealthy Connections

Heavenly Father,

I come before You acknowledging that You are the only one who can break every ungodly soul tie and unhealthy connection in my life. I repent for any soul ties formed with people, places, or situations not of You. I renounce any emotional, spiritual, or physical bond established outside of Your will.

In the name of Jesus, I break every soul tie that has kept me in bondage, whether it be through unhealthy relationships, past trauma, or spiritual compromise. I command every tie to be severed and declare that my heart, mind, and soul are free in Jesus' name.

Holy Spirit, heal every area where I've been wounded or bound by these connections. I release forgiveness over every person and situation I've been tied to, and I choose to walk in the freedom and peace You have for me. Thank you, Father, for healing my soul and setting me free.

In Jesus' name, Amen.

9. Prayer for Releasing and Restoring God's Peace

Lord of Peace,

I thank You for the peace that surpasses all understanding **(Philippians 4:7)**. I come before You asking that You would release Your perfect peace into every area of my life. I renounce the spirit of anxiety, fear, and worry that has tried to take control. I command every unsettled spirit to leave now in the name of Jesus.

Holy Spirit, flood my heart and mind with peace. Restore the calm in my spirit, and help me to rest in Your presence. Let Your peace reign in my relationships, finances, health, and mind. I choose to trust You with every situation, knowing that You will give me peace that nothing and no one can take away.

In Jesus' name, Amen.

10. Prayer for Personal Healing and Restoration

Father God,

I come before You, trusting in Your power to heal and restore. I ask you to heal every area of my life—physically, emotionally, and spiritually. I lay before You every wound, every hurt, and every broken part of me that needs restoration. I surrender my pain and my past into Your hands.

By Jesus' stripes, I declare that I am healed **(Isaiah 53:5)**. I ask You to heal my body from sickness, restore my emotions from hurt, and renew my spirit to be strong in You. Remove any bitterness, anger, or unforgiveness from my heart and replace it with Your love and peace.

In Jesus' name, Amen.

11. Prayer for Breaking the Spirit of Rejection

Heavenly Father,

I thank you for accepting me and calling me your child. I repent for any areas where I have allowed the spirit of rejection to take root in my life. I renounce every lie that I am unworthy, unwanted, or unloved. I declare that I am accepted in the Beloved and belong to You (Ephesians 1:6).

In Jesus' name, I break the power of rejection off my life and declare that I no longer receive the spirit of rejection. I command every hurt from past rejections to leave now. I invite Your love and acceptance to flood my heart, and I stand firm in my identity as Your child.

Thank you, Lord, for Your love and acceptance.

In Jesus' name, Amen.

12. Prayer for Freedom from Addiction and Strongholds

Lord Jesus,

I come before You, asking for freedom from every addiction and stronghold in my life. I declare that you have come to set the captives free **(Luke 4:18)**, and I claim that freedom today. I renounce any addictions, whether to substances, habits, or behaviors, and I break every chain that has held me in bondage. I command every spirit of addiction to leave my life now in the name of Jesus. I declare I can walk in Your righteousness, peace, and joy. Fill me with the Holy Spirit, and empower me to resist every temptation and live according to Your will.

Thank You, Father, for delivering me and setting me free.

In Jesus' name, Amen.

13. Prayer for Protection Against Spiritual Attacks

Father God,

I thank You for being my refuge and fortress (Psalm 91:2). I come to You today asking for divine protection over my life, family, and home. I declare that no weapon formed against me shall prosper, and every spiritual attack is defeated in the name of Jesus.

I ask you to place a hedge of protection around me, my loved ones, and all that pertains to me. Surround me with Your angels, and keep me safe from physical, emotional, or spiritual attacks. I trust in Your power to shield me from all evil and to keep me safe in Your arms.

In Jesus' name, Amen.

14. Prayer for Revival and Spiritual Awakening

Lord Jesus,

I come before You with a hunger for revival in my heart. I ask You to awaken my spirit and set my heart ablaze with a desire to know You more. Let the fire of Your presence fall upon me, bringing transformation, renewal, and a fresh outpouring of Your Holy Spirit.

Revive every area of my life that has grown cold, and ignite a passion for Your Word, Your will, and Your work. I declare that I will be a vessel of revival in my community, family, and church. Use me to bring light into dark places and to spread your love to those who need it most.

In Jesus' name, Amen.

15. Prayer for Receiving God's Promises and Provision

Father God,

I thank you for your abundant provision in my life. Your Word declares that You will supply all of my needs according to Your riches in glory **(Philippians 4:19)**. I come before You today, trusting You to provide for every area of my life—physically, financially, and spiritually.

I declare that I will lack nothing good, and I stand in the fullness of Your promises. I ask You to open the doors of provision and breakthrough, and I receive the blessings You have prepared for me. I trust your perfect timing and faithfulness to provide for all my needs.

Thank you, Lord, for Your provision and promises that never fail.

In Jesus' name, Amen.

16. Prayer for Breaking Bloodline Curses

Father, in the name of Jesus,

I come before You acknowledging the bloodline curses passed down through my family. I renounce every curse of failure, poverty, sickness, addiction, and bondage that has been operating in my family line.

I declare that I am free from every generational curse by the blood of Jesus Christ. I break every legal right the enemy has gained through past iniquities, and I declare that the cycle of destruction stops here. I speak blessings, healing, and prosperity into my bloodline.

In the name of Jesus, I am free, and my family is free.

Amen.

17. Prayer for Renouncing Demonic Altars

In the name of Jesus,

I renounce every demonic altar operating in my life. I break the power of every altar raised against me, my family, and my destiny. I sever all covenants, vows, and agreements made with the enemy and declare that they are null and void.

I plead the blood of Jesus over my life, and I command every demonic structure to be destroyed by the fire of God. I stand in the authority of Jesus Christ and declare that I am free from every influence of demonic altars. I establish God's altar in my life, family, and home, inviting His presence to dwell in every area.

In Jesus' name,

Amen.

18. Prayer for Deliverance from Fear and Anxiety

Father, in the name of Jesus,

I come against every spirit of fear and anxiety that is tormenting me. Your Word says that You have not given me a spirit of fear but of power, love, and a sound mind (2 Timothy 1:7).

I break the spirit of fear off my life now. I cancel every lie of the enemy that has caused me to live in fear, worry, and anxiety. I speak peace to my heart and mind and invite Your perfect peace to fill me.

I take authority over every spirit of fear and declare that I am free in Jesus' name.

Amen.

19. Prayer for Deliverance from Oppression and Affliction

Father, in the mighty name of Jesus,

I come before You seeking deliverance from every form of oppression and affliction weighing me down. I recognize that Jesus came to set the captives free, and I declare that I am no longer a captive to oppression or affliction. I break every chain the enemy has placed upon my mind, body, or spirit.

I command every demonic spirit that is causing oppression, fear, sickness, or despair to leave my life now in Jesus' name. I receive the fullness of Your healing, peace, and deliverance today.

Amen.

20. Prayer for Breaking Soul Ties

Father, in the name of Jesus,

I come before You and repent for any ungodly soul ties I have formed. I break every emotional, spiritual, and physical tie that does not align with your will. I sever all unhealthy connections from my past, including those tied to people, places, or situations.

I declare that these soul ties are broken, and I am free from any lingering emotional or spiritual attachments. I ask You to cleanse my soul, heal my heart, and restore my identity in You.

Thank You for setting me free. In Jesus' name,

Amen.

APPENDIX B
Quick Reference Prophetic Declarations & Activation Prayers

Prophetic Declaration:

I decree and declare that the fire of God dismantles every demonic altar erected against my life, destiny, and bloodline. I prophesy divine reversal over every curse, cycle, and covenant that once held me captive. I am no longer a prisoner of my past, of ancestral covenants, or hidden altars—I am a child of God, redeemed by the blood of Jesus.

I declare that generational curses are broken. Patterns of delay, barrenness, failure, and sickness are overturned. I walk in divine alignment, supernatural acceleration, and kingdom authority. From this moment forward, I operate under the influence of godly altars of fire, purity, worship, and divine covenant.

I am a generational altar breaker. I am a territory taker. I am a bloodline restorer. The anointing upon my life will speak louder than the altars of my past. My future is secure in Christ, and my freedom is non-negotiable.

Activation Prayer:

Heavenly Father,

I step into the courtroom of Heaven and bring every demonic altar that has spoken against my life into divine judgment. I present the blood of Jesus as evidence and silence every accusation from the enemy. Let the fire of God fall now and consume every ungodly altar—altars of poverty, affliction, delay, trauma, addiction, perversion, and idolatry.

I revoke every legal right the enemy has gained through my bloodline, knowingly or unknowingly. I renounce the sins of my ancestors and declare that their agreements no longer stand over me. I establish a new altar—an altar of righteousness, worship, holiness, and divine access to the throne of God.

Holy Spirit, activate every word of this chapter in my spirit. Let it not fall to the ground, but produce fruit that remains. Teach my hands to war and my fingers to fight. Reveal hidden altars. Expose ancient foundations. Empower me with wisdom, fire, and discernment to stand in victory.

From this day forward, I walk in unshakable freedom.

In Jesus' mighty and matchless name—Amen!

Prophetic Declaration:

I declare that I have been given authority in Christ Jesus to break every legal claim and dismantle every demonic altar that stands against my destiny. I am free from the legal rights of the enemy, and I walk in the fullness of God's divine order. I proclaim that no weapon formed against me shall prosper, and every spiritual claim made by the enemy is now rendered invalid by the blood of Jesus.

I declare that generational curses or iniquities do not bind my life, family, or future. The enemy no longer has legal access to my life through sin, covenants, or agreements. I stand in the authority of Christ and declare that every demonic altar raised against me is dismantled, broken, and utterly destroyed in the name of Jesus.

I decree that I am now aligned with God's divine order, walking in victory, peace, and freedom. My past is washed clean, and every legal claim established through sin or unrepentant actions is erased. I declare that I will walk in unshakable authority, releasing God's power to dismantle every stronghold that has held me captive.

Activation Prayer:

Father, in Jesus' name,

I thank You for revealing the spiritual legalities that have bound me and my family. I repent of any sins, covenants, or agreements I or my ancestors have made with the enemy, knowingly or unknowingly. I break every ungodly covenant, every word spoken in agreement with darkness, and every ritual that has empowered demonic altars in my life.

I stand before You as Your chosen vessel, cleansed by the blood of Jesus. I renounce the legal rights the enemy has had in my life, and I claim the victory of the Cross. I break every curse, every tie to generational iniquity, and I command every demonic spirit tied to past altars to leave in the mighty name of Jesus.

Lord, I declare that your divine order will now govern my life. Your Holy Spirit has come to dwell in every area of my being, and I give You full authority to take control over every area the enemy once held sway over. I declare that I am free to walk in my destiny, in victory, and in the fullness of Your blessings.

I now declare that every demonic altar, every legal claim, and every stronghold is completely demolished. I stand on the Word of God and the authority of Jesus Christ and proclaim that the enemy's power is broken.

Thank you, Lord, for setting me free. In Jesus' name, I pray. Amen.

Prophetic Declaration:

I declare that every demonic altar that has been established in my life and family line is dismantled now by the power of the blood of Jesus Christ. I break every chain, every stronghold, and every legal right the enemy has used to bind me. I stand in the authority of Jesus and declare that every altar of darkness must fall.

I decree that the power of generational iniquities, sinful covenants, and demonic agreements is now null and void. No altar, personal or ancestral, has the right to bind me or my descendants. I declare that I am free from every form of spiritual bondage, including spiritual, mental, emotional, physical, financial, and territorial chains.

I command every demonic altar that has been erected to sabotage my destiny, health, and peace to be consumed by the fire of God. I declare that I enter a new season of freedom, prosperity, and divine alignment with God's will. The altars of darkness no longer have authority over me, for the blood of Jesus covers me.

Activation Prayer:

Father, in the name of Jesus, I thank You for revealing the truth about the demonic altars that have bound me and my family. I repent for every sin, agreement, and covenant that has given legal ground to the enemy. I renounce every tie to demonic altars and the strongholds they've built in my life. I cancel every curse, vow, or sacrifice that has empowered these altars.

I break every generational iniquity, every family curse, and every demonic covenant that has been passed down to me. I declare that no altar—whether formed through my actions, the actions of my ancestors, or any other means—has the right to influence my life, health, finances, or destiny.

Lord, I invite Your Holy Spirit to fill every area of my life where these altars once held sway. I ask You to restore what the enemy has stolen and establish Your divine order and peace. I receive Your freedom, Your healing, and Your breakthrough.

I now activate my authority in Christ Jesus and decree that every demonic altar is broken, destroyed, and consumed by the fire of God. I declare that the legal claims of the enemy are forever nullified, and I walk forward in the power of Your truth. No longer will I be held captive by these altars, but I am free to fulfill the destiny You have ordained for me.

I thank You, Father, for the victory in Jesus' name. Amen.

Prophetic Declaration:

I declare today that I am walking in the authority and power given to me through Jesus Christ. I stand as a child of the Most High God, free from every demonic altar, every ancestral curse, and every spiritual stronghold. I break the chains that have held me, my family, and my bloodline captive. I declare that every altar of darkness that has influenced my life is now dismantled in the name of Jesus.

I proclaim freedom over my life, health, finances, and future. No longer will I be bound by recurring cycles of failure, sickness, or oppression. I declare that the blood of Jesus Christ nullifies the power of every demonic altar.

I renounce every generational sin, every vow, and every covenant made with the kingdom of darkness. I proclaim that the legal rights of the enemy to operate in my life are revoked by the authority of Jesus' name. My family is free from every ancestral stronghold; we walk in divine freedom and victory.

I declare that God's kingdom is advancing in my life. Through my prayers, worship, and obedience to God, I now build a Godly altar. I invite His presence into every area of my life and commit myself and my family to Him.

Activation Prayer:

Father, in Jesus' name, I activate the power and authority You have given me. I declare that I am free from the influence of demonic altars in my life and bloodline. I repent of any sins or agreements made knowingly or unknowingly that have empowered these altars. I renounce every generational curse and covenant passed down through my family line.

By the blood of Jesus, I break every legal claim the enemy has held over my life. I speak to every altar of darkness and declare that it has no more power, influence, or legal right to operate in my life. I decree that the blood of Jesus covers every part of me spirit, soul, and body and I am made whole.

I activate the power of God's Word in my life and speak life, prosperity, health, and victory into every area where darkness once had control. I stand firm in my authority as a child of God, and I declare that my family is free, my life is free, and I will walk in the fullness of the freedom and blessing You have prepared for me.

Holy Spirit, I invite You to take complete control of my life. Establish your presence in every room of my heart, and fill me with the power to walk in complete victory. I build a godly altar through prayers, worship, and obedience to You.

In Jesus' mighty name, I pray. Amen.

What's Next on Your Journey to Freedom?

Congratulations on completing The Altar Breaker: Unlocking the Secret to Deliverance and Spiritual Freedom. You've taken a bold step toward spiritual healing, breaking generational curses, and walking in the authority God has given you. But this is only the beginning.

Deliverance is not just a moment—it's a lifestyle. It's a continual process of healing, renewing your mind, and building godly altars in place of the ones you've destroyed. I want to personally invite you to go deeper.

Here's how you can continue your journey:

Book a 1-on-1 Prophetic Consultation, Coaching and Deliverance: Receive personal prayer, strategy, and guidance tailored to your spiritual season.

Coming soon:

The Altar Breaker Community: A safe place for support, mentorship, and next-level training in spiritual warfare and prophetic activation.

School of Deliverance & Prophetic Training: Gain deeper understanding of the spirit realm and be equipped to walk in your full calling.

Let's Stay Connected

Website: www.MonicaLaRelle.com

Email: info@iammonicalarelle.com

Instagram: @iam.monicalarelle

Facebook: IamMonicalarelle

Tiktok: Iam.monicalarelle

Want to share your testimony from this book?

Submit your story: info@iammonicalarelle.com

Thank you for allowing me to walk with you through this journey.

You were born to break altars and build legacies. Keep pressing forward.

www.ingramcontent.com/pod-product-compliance
Lightning Source LLC
Chambersburg PA
CBHW072131160426
43197CB00012B/2069